Growing up as an exile in Switzerland, Louis Napoleon Bonaparte, nephew of the great Napoleon, was determined to re-establish the glory of the French Empire. On finally becoming Emperor, after two abortive invasions, he chose Eugénie, a red-haired, fiery Spanish beauty, to be his Empress. Their relationship was tempestuous but ultimately happy in their final years spent, once again, in exile.

HEIR TO A FAMOUS NAME

FIRED BY STORIES ABOUT THE GREAT NAPOLEON I, YOUNG LOUIS NAPOLEON WOULD BECOME HEIR TO AN EMPIRE THAT NO LONGER EXISTED. BUT HE HAD PLANS TO CHANGE THAT

Roger-Viollet/Musee Marmottan

Bridgeman/Crown Estate Commissions, London

LOUIS NAPOLEON BONAPARTE WAS BORN ON 20 April 1808. He was the third son of Louis Bonaparte, who was the younger brother of Napoleon I, and of Louis' wife, Hortense de Beauharnais. Not only was the young Louis the nephew of Napoleon I, but he was also the grandson of Joséphine de Beauharnais, Napoleon I's first wife. He came from a distinguished family and was heir to an illustrious name.

Hortense de Beauharnais' marriage to Louis Bonaparte had not been a success. She was lively, pretty and outgoing, she enjoyed painting and had a considerable talent for composing songs. One of her compositions, '*Partant pour la Syrie*' would become the unofficial anthem of France under the Empire of her son. Her husband, who rarely enjoyed good

♛ *Louis' mother Hortense* above left *was both step-daughter and sister-in-law to Napoleon Bonaparte. Her marriage to Napoleon's younger brother made her, temporarily, Queen of Holland*

♛ *Napoleon Bonaparte* above *dominated Europe as Emperor of France, while his brothers ruled in Spain, Westphalia and Holland. However, all his efforts to found a dynasty met with failure*

health, was jealous and morose. In 1810, after quarrelling with his brother, Napoleon I, over how he should rule the Kingdom of Holland and how he should treat Hortense, he abdicated his throne and was divorced.

Paternity doubts

There was always some doubt as to the paternity of Louis Napoleon, who was born a month prematurely. Gossip-mongers claimed that Hortense had simply invented the story of his premature birth in order to make the dates fit. Among the putative fathers suggested for the young Prince was Napoleon himself.

The story was almost certainly a slanderous lie, although Napoleon was always very fond of Hortense. When he escaped from Elba, he had no Empress to stand by him during the 100 days that led up to the Battle of Waterloo – Joséphine had died and his second wife, Marie Louise, had returned to Austria. Hortense, therefore, moved into the Tuileries with her two surviving sons (the eldest had died in childhood) and acted as hostess for him.

After Waterloo, Hortense was banished from France and, what was worse, her husband claimed custody of their elder son, Napoleon Louis, who went to live with his father in Florence. Hortense eventually settled in Switzerland, buying a château overlooking Lake Constance. It was there at Arenenberg, in beautiful, romantic woodland, that Louis Napoleon spent most of his childhood.

A good pupil

Hortense was an indulgent mother to the one son in her care. While she filled his imagination with tales of Napoleon and Joséphine, his tutor had great difficulty in getting him to concentrate on his schoolwork. Louis was a likeable child, but he tended to be lazy and a daydreamer.

All this changed when, in 1820, Hortense engaged a new tutor – Philippe Le Bas, son of an artisan who had been a prominent supporter of Robespierre in the Revolution. Le Bas himself was an unshakeable republican; his lessons, even those in Latin and Greek, dealt at length with questions of social justice, a subject that appealed to the idealistic Louis. Le Bas imposed a strict new timetable on his pupil, transforming him into an early riser and a voracious reader, keen to make his mark in the world as a writer and political thinker.

A German education

The following year Louis was sent as a day-boy to the Gymnasium at Augsburg, where Hortense had a winter residence. There, despite the disadvantage of being taught in German, he soon rose to be fourth in the class. His French,

Roger-Viollet

however, acquired a slight German accent that he never succeeded in losing.

Over the next few years Louis was able to see more of his father and brother in Rome, where there were regular gatherings of the Bonaparte clan. He looked up to his dashing elder brother as a natural leader. Few people would have tipped the shorter, far less attractive Louis for greatness. He had been a delicate child, but at Arenenberg had become a bold swimmer and a good horseman.

When the time came for Louis to become a soldier, he did not take to it willingly, but disciplined himself to make a thorough study of

♔ *Young Louis* above, *the third son of one of Napoleon's younger brothers, was never regarded as the heir to the Emperor's dynastic ambitions. His early years were full of turmoil and upheaval as political change and his parents' divorce kept his family on the move around Europe*

A DYNASTY IN EXILE

When Napoleon was exiled to St Helena in 1815 *right*, members of his family were not treated as harshly as he, but all were banished from France. Napoleon's son, the King of Rome, had been taken to Vienna by his mother. He was brought up as an Austrian Prince but on Napoleon's death, in 1821, loyal Bonapartists considered him to be the rightful Emperor of France – Napoleon II. He died of tuberculosis in 1832, aged 21.

Of Napoleon's brothers, one, Joseph, ex-King of Naples, settled in New Jersey, America. The other three lived in Italy: Lucien in Rome, Jerome in Trieste and Louis, the father of the future Napoleon III, in Florence

Mary Evans

Both pictures: Roger-Viollet

👑 *When her mother, Josephine, died in 1814, Hortense inherited the Château at Pregny, in Savoy top. She and Louis lived there briefly after the Battle of Waterloo, but they were hounded out of France and settled eventually in Switzerland, at the Château of Arenenberg, in the woods near Lausanne above*

artillery at the Swiss officers' academy at Thun. He joined in the typical pursuits of young men of his age with enthusiasm, so much so that a visiting Englishman saw him as a 'wild harum-scarum youth ...riding at full gallop through the streets to the peril of the public, fencing and pistol shooting, and apparently without serious thought of any kind.'

To Hortense Cornu, a girl who had grown up with him in his mother's household, Louis confided, 'I can be happy in my own way in-

stead of being, as the head of our house must be, the slave of a mission.' The events of the years 1831 and 1832 put an end to this brief period of carefree irresponsibility.

Italian escapade

The two brothers were persuaded to join the Carbonari, the secret association that hoped to unite Italy as an independent country. They fought bravely in skirmishes with the Papal troops, but when a huge Austrian army started to march southwards, it became clear that the revolutionaries had no hope of success. Nevertheless the brothers decided to make their way across country to Ancona where they expected the final battle to take place. On the way Napoleon Louis fell ill and died of measles.

The older Bonapartes in no way approved

'A wild harum-scarum youth...apparently without serious thought'

COMMENT ON LOUIS, AGED 20

of the young brothers' crazy escapade, but, when Hortense heard that her son was ill, she got hold of false British passports and set off to the rescue. She was too late to save her elder son, but showed astonishing courage and resourcefulness in saving Louis Napoleon from the marauding Austrian armies.

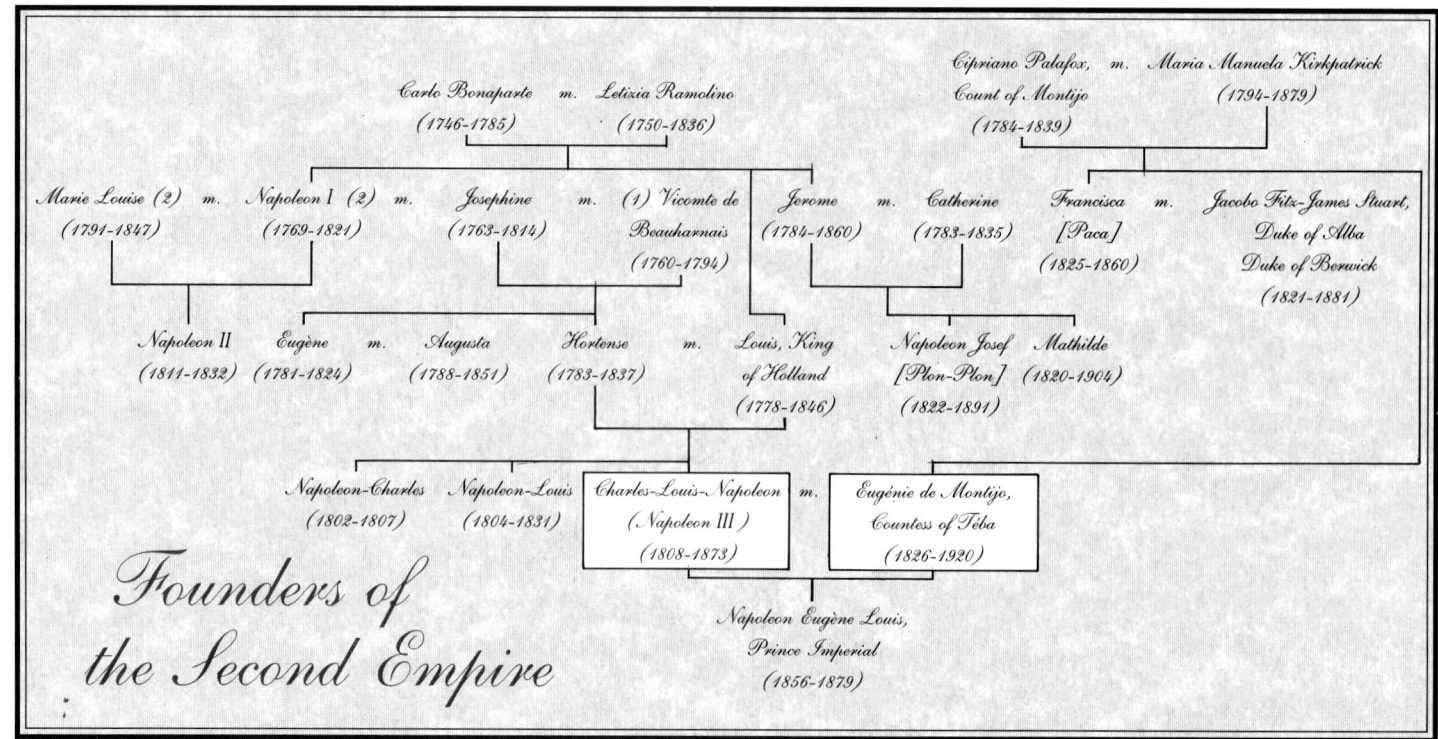

Founders of the Second Empire

First she had to hide him while nursing him through a week of violent fever – he had caught measles from his brother. There followed a cloak-and-dagger coach-ride across Italy with Louis disguised as a footman, then as an English gentleman. The madcap journey continued into France; they made their way undetected – despite the fact that Hortense spoke no English and Louis' knowledge of it was far from perfect – as far as Paris, where Louis fell ill again.

Hortense announced her presence by secret messenger to King Louis Philippe, who granted them safe conduct provided they did not make their exploit public. The adventure ended in England, where Whig aristocrats were happy to invite them into their homes and

Reunion Musees Nationaux

MATHILDE BONAPARTE

Unlike her younger brother, Prince Napoleon, Mathilde *above* never played an active part in politics. As a girl, her one aim in life was to return to Paris, 'that wonderful Paris . . .the theatre in which the founder of our glorious dynasty held the stage.' She got her wish in 1840, when she married a Russian Prince, Anatole Demidov, and the couple were made welcome in France by King Louis Philippe.

Although her marriage was a disaster, Mathilde soon established herself as the hostess of the most glittering literary salon in Paris. When her cousin, Louis Napoleon, became Emperor, he is said to have proposed marriage to her again – nearly 20 years after the idea had first been discussed. But she preferred her life as a patroness of the arts

Roger-Viollet

good-looking women welcomed the amorous attentions of the romantic and mysterious young Bonaparte.

Changing his appearance

It was in England that Louis first grew the ends of his moustache and had them waxed and curled. However, a Miss Godfrey of Tunbridge Wells, whom he was trying to impress, objected to them and he had to cut them off. In later years his extravagant moustaches and 'imperial' beard became a mask behind which he could conceal his true emotions. He would also keep his eyelids half-closed as he spoke to people, which gave him a strange far-away dreamy look. This was a deliberate ploy to put people off their guard.

Hortense Cornu noticed the start of this kind of behaviour when he returned to

♛ *While Louis spent his childhood with his mother in Switzerland, his elder brother, Napoleon Louis, lived in Florence with his father, Louis Bonaparte above. The brothers met only occasionally during their childhood, usually in Rome, where the whole Bonaparte family gathered for reunions*

Arenenberg: 'I cannot better describe the change that came over him after his brother's death than by saying he tore his heart out of his bosom and surrendered himself to his head.'

Louis may have gained mastery of his heart, but there were other parts of the body that he found difficult to control. When he resumed his life as an artillery captain in Switzerland, his 'amours' with the local female population became quite scandalous.

'He tore his heart out of his bosom and surrendered himself to his head'

HORTENSE CORNU ON LOUIS

They were seldom the sort of women he could consider marrying; his thoughts to the future were directed towards his new-found political ambition. His mother, worried about his health rather than his morals, eventually decided it might be time to find him a wife.

Coquettish cousin

Members of the scattered Bonaparte family could see the dynastic advantages of a marriage between Louis and his cousin, Princess Mathilde, the daughter of Jerome Bonaparte, Napoleon I's youngest brother. In 1836, Jerome, who had been King of Westphalia under the Empire, came with his three children to stay at Arenenberg. Hortense and Jerome tentatively discussed the political and financial aspects of the match, but allowed Louis and Mathilde to enjoy each other's company without placing them under any obligations.

Mathilde, though not yet sixteen, certainly knew what was expected of her, doing all she could to inflame Louis' passion. Valérie Masuyer, one of Hortense's ladies-in-waiting, describes a typical scene at the dinner table: 'When I arrived for dinner I found her father grumbling at her for being too décolletée. He was right: she was revealing too much. But everything she displayed was so beautiful that it was a pleasure to behold. The Prince was quite struck and devoured her with his eyes. With him the flesh is weak.'

A certain amount of flirtation and hand-holding took place and there were tears on departure, but Louis had another plan more important for the moment than marriage – a revolution in France.

Mary Evans

Louis' accomplices in this, his first serious bid for power, were an ex-soldier, journalist and adventurer, who called himself the Comte de Persigny, and a fashionable singer, Eléonore Gordon, the widow of an English officer. People claimed that she was Louis' mistress, but this was unlikely – Louis usually kept business and pleasure strictly separate.

March on Paris

Their plan was simple: the French army was full of officers who had fought under Napoleon; they would present themselves to the garrison at Strasbourg, win over the officers and men and march on Paris, gathering support as they went. The one high-ranking accomplice they had in Strasbourg, Colonel Vaudrey, had been recruited, not because he had any confidence in Louis Napoleon, but because he wanted to sleep with Eléonore Gordon.

Vaudrey's own regiment, the 4th Artillery, was easily won over – it had been the great Napoleon's own regiment as a young artillery officer. But when Louis appeared at the barracks of the 46th Infantry Regiment, dressed in a colonel's uniform with just a few of his supporters, the commanding officer denounced him as an impostor and had him arrested.

Astonishingly, Louis was not tried for his crime – perhaps because no blood had been shed during the farcical proceedings. He was simply put on a ship and deported to the United States. While the ship made a long detour via Rio de Janeiro, his accomplices were tried – and acquitted!

Newspapers all over Europe dismissed the attempted coup as 'pathetic', 'absurd' and 'con-

♔ *With the death of his brother, from measles, in 1831, closely followed by that of his cousin, Napoleon II, in 1832, young Louis* above *found himself the oldest surviving male Bonaparte of his generation, with all the dynasty's hopes vested in him*

♔ *Eugénie's mother, Manuela* below *was part Belgian, part Scottish. She was a heady mixture of ambition and beauty, with a sociable nature and a generous disposition*

Mas

Bridgeman

temptible.' Nobody, it appeared, had the slightest faith in the young man's destiny. Ex-King Jerome immediately scotched the idea of his marrying Mathilde, forbidding her even to write to him in America.

A future Empress

It was to be a long time before Louis would contemplate marriage again. The woman who would take her place at his side, when he finally realized his dream of becoming Emperor, was just ten years old when Louis was deported to America. She would become known as Eugénie, but she was christened Maria Eugénia Ignacia Augustina de Guzman y Palafox. She had been born in Grenada, Spain on 5 May 1826, during an earthquake. To avoid the danger of falling masonry, her mother, Maria Manuela, gave birth to her in a tent erected in the garden.

Eugénie's father, Don Cipriano, Count of Teba, was a battle-scarred veteran of the Napoleonic Wars. He had a wounded arm and leg, received in the Emperor's service, and also wore a black patch over a missing eye. In 1817 he had married Maria Manuela Kirkpatrick, the beautiful, young, ambitious daughter of a Scottish wine-merchant with a flourishing business in Malaga.

Temperamentally, Eugénie's parents were just as unsuited as Louis Napoleon's had been. Manuela was generous, extravagant and flirtatious; she loved society, particularly the company of witty literary men. Don Cipriano, accustomed to the rigours of military campaigns, preferred a simple, frugal life away from the luxury and chatter of courts and salons.

The title 'de Montijo,' which the French la-

👑 *Eugénie was born in the ancient city of Granada above in Andalusia. Her father had been exiled from Madrid owing to his support for Napoleon against the repressive Spanish Royal Family*

'With him the flesh is weak'

MME MASUYER ON LOUIS

Roger-Viollet

👑 *The mystery of Eugénie's parentage was mischievously fostered by Manuela herself, who was rumoured to have had an affair with George Villiers, later Earl of Clarendon above*

ter mistook for Eugénie's family name, belonged to Cipriano's elder brother, Eugenio, a rich old bachelor. When the old count was lured into marriage by an adventuress, Manuela was concerned that they might have children who would inherit the title and the money which would otherwise go to her husband.

Fortunately for Manuela, Eugenio suffered a stroke, which left him partially paralysed and most unlikely to sire an heir. His wife, however, faked a pregnancy and obtained an orphan boy to present to the world as her legitimate son.

The fortune-hunter foiled

Manuela, who was at the time banished from Madrid, charmed the King into relaxing this restriction on her movements and hurried to her brother-in-law's house in the capital to unmask the plot. One version of the story has her marching into the lady's bedroom and throwing back the bedclothes to reveal the deception. Thus, when Eugenio died in 1834, Cipriano inherited the title and Manuela became Countess de Montijo.

For all Manuela's desire to protect her husband's rightful inheritance, the birth of her own daughters aroused a great deal of speculation about dates and legitimacy. Manuela's carefree morals gave rise to many rumours about Eugénie's parentage that would plague her when she became Empress.

The man who might have been Eugénie's father was an Englishman, George Villiers, who became Earl of Clarendon and Foreign Secretary under Queen Victoria. He was almost certainly Manuela's lover in Madrid a few years after Eugénie was born.

IMPERIAL TREASURE TROVE

Napoleon III added little to the existing Crown Jewels of France, but he did have several new pieces made for the Empress. Eugénie's personal collection was fabulous, probably unrivalled in Europe; an auction of these in 1872 helped to support the imperial family in exile. For political rather than financial reasons, most of the Crown Jewels were sold in 1887

♛ This magnificent brooch *left*, remodelled for the Empress Eugénie contains in the centre two fabulous Mazarin diamonds, first cut and mounted for Louis XIV. It was one of the few pieces not sold in the sale of 1887

Archiv für Kunst & Geschichte

Courtesy, Mercatorfonds NV

♛ Napoleon III displays all the trappings of Empire in this portrait *above*. The Imperial Crown on the cushion is not accurately represented by the artist, except for the famous Regent diamond at its top. This is one of the purest and brightest diamonds in the world and, like Eugénie's brooch, escaped the sale of 1887 and can now be seen in the Louvre

♛ Both the drop pearl and four-stringed necklace worn by Eugenie in this portrait were part of the Crown Jewels

Ballot

Courtesy, Mercatorfonds NV/Musee Carnavalet

Roger-Viollet Chateau Compiegne

♛ This brooch in silver and gold has a ruby and sapphire centre depicting the arms of the city of Paris and is decorated with diamonds and pearls *above*. It was given to Empress Eugénie by the city of Paris to mark the birth of her son

Courtesy, Mercatorfonds NV/Private Collection

♛ In this splendid portrait by Winterhalter *above* Eugénie wears the pearls that form part of the Crown Jewels – the diadem *left*, coronet and eight-string pearl necklace. The diadem and coronet, which were especially made for her by the jeweller, Lemonnier, in the year of her marriage, were sold by the State in 1887 to private collectors, and fetched the considerable sums of 100,000 and 30,000 francs respectively

COQUETTE AND SEDUCER

AS EUGÉNIE GREW UP, LOUIS PLANNED ANOTHER INVASION. HE WAS IMPRISONED BUT ESCAPED AND, AFTER THE 1848 REVOLUTION, BECAME PRESIDENT OF FRANCE. HE THEN MET EUGÉNIE FOR THE FIRST TIME

Roger-Viollet

♔ *In 1830, a new, slightly more liberal regime allowed Don Cipriano to return to Madrid. His wife and daughters spent a good deal of time in Paris, then enjoying a period of relative stability. There, in 1837, a family portrait above was painted, with the absent Don Cipriano represented by a painting*

♔ *After seven years of virtual house arrest, Don Cipriano liked nothing better than to ride through the countryside and villages of Southern Spain right. Eugénie accompanied him from a very early age. She learned to love her country and the outdoor life while listening to her father's tales of Bonaparte*

E UGENIE WAS BROUGHT UP IN THE CONS-tant company of her sister, Francisca, who was always known as Paca. The two were very close, although Eugé-nie seemed to seek Paca's friendship more than Paca sought hers, but they were very different in appearance and character. Paca, 15 months older than Eugénie, was dark, gentle and, ex-cept when encouraged by her sister, obedient and docile. Eugénie was red-haired, blue-eyed, rebellious and distinctly tomboyish.

A story that became part of family folklore recounts how, having learnt from somewhere that girls became boys by falling downstairs, Eugénie threw herself down the staircase of the family home in Madrid.

While Paca was more attached to her mother, Eugénie loved the tales told by her father of his battles in the colours of the Emper-or Napoleon. She also loved riding long dis-tances with him through the wild Spanish countryside.

Although Cipriano and Manuela had little in common, each seems to have accepted the other's different tastes and opinions without quarrels and recriminations. Eugénie was al-ways happiest when all four members of the family could be together under the same roof. This, sadly, was rarely the case.

Don Cipriano's fortunes revived greatly with the death of Ferdinand VII in 1833 and his inheritance of the Montijo titles, lands and houses in the following year. He became a sena-tor in the Spanish Parliament, but the civil war between rival contenders for the Spanish crown made Spain a dangerous place to live. In 1834 a terrible cholera epidemic added to the country's turmoil. Cipriano agreed that it would be prudent for Manuela to take the girls to the safety of Paris.

Sketchy education

The girls' education was sketchy and frequent-ly interrupted. They acquired most of their knowledge of the world through contact with their mother's literary friends — in particular the cynical Prosper Mérimée, who had become a close friend of the family on a visit to Spain a few years before.

Mérimée introduced the girls to the great writer Stendhal, who was working on *La Char-treuse de Parme*. The novel contains a cele-brated account of the Battle of Waterloo. Sten-dhal must have tried out the effect of his de-

Fine Art Photographic

The family's wandering existence came to an end in 1839 when Don Cipriano died. Manuela hurried back to his deathbed, but the girls were left in Paris to follow on later. They were not told of his death until they arrived in Madrid. The 13-year-old Eugénie did not cry; she shut herself in her room and refused to speak to anyone for two days.

If the year 1839 marked a tragic turning point in Eugénie's childhood, 1840 was the lowest point in Louis Napoleon's chequered career. After the disaster of Strasbourg he had

'What do I care for the cries of the mob'

LOUIS TO HIS MOTHER

refused to be disheartened. A letter to his mother from America reveals a stoic indifference to failure: 'What do I care for the cries of the mob, who will call me mad because I have failed, and who would have exaggerated my merits if I had succeeded.'

When he arrived in New York, he was feted as a champion of liberty in the Land of the Free. In June 1837 he was planning a tour of the Mid-West and Canada, when he received a letter from Hortense begging him to return to Arenenberg. She had cancer.

Louis sailed to Liverpool, then, with the aid of a friend's American passport, managed to cross Europe to Switzerland. He spent two sad, but very affectionate months with his mother

scription on his young Spanish friends, for the manuscript contains a cryptic footnote that has been deciphered as 'For you, Paca and Eugénie, 15 December 1838'.

Their father would have approved of the Napoleonic history his daughters learned from Stendhal, but he was worried that they might become too accustomed to their mother's luxurious lifestyle. When he stayed with them in Paris for the summer of 1835, he insisted, according to Mérimée, that they wore simple linen dresses and that they should walk or ride, instead of travelling in their mother's carriage. He also forbade them to carry an umbrella when it rained. He reinforced this rather spartan regime by sending them to the Gymnase Normal, a school that offered physical education to pupils of both sexes.

The sisters' varied education also included two months at a boarding school in Clifton, in Bristol, during a visit by Manuela to England. On their return to Paris, they brought with them an English governess, Miss Flowers, who would remain with the family for over half a century. She was, however, quite incapable of disciplining the girls, especially the strong-willed Eugénie, during Maria Manuela's frequent absences.

Eugénie was never happy at any of the schools she attended. Wherever she went, she was teased on account of her red hair and she missed her father terribly. Her one friend at Clifton was a home-sick Indian Princess, for whom she felt a great sympathy. The two of them were discovered at Bristol Docks, trying to stow away on a ship bound for India.

☙ *In 1834 a cholera epidemic added to the woes of Spain, which was already racked by civil war. In Madrid, reactionary monks were thought to have caused the disease by poisoning the wells. Eugénie watched in horror from the family home as the church across the way was attacked by an angry mob* above, *and a monk stabbed to death in the street*

PROSPER MÉRIMÉE

French writers of the Romantic period were fascinated by the drama and colour of Spanish life. This foreigners' view of Spain was embodied in Prosper Mérimée's short novel *Carmen*, which became the source of Bizet's celebrated opera. On a trip to Spain in 1830, the young Mérimée met Eugénie's mother, Manuela, and they became life-long friends, though never, as was rumoured, lovers. *Carmen* was based on a story she told him.

Mérimée *right* played the role of kindly uncle to Manuela's daughters in Paris. Having known Eugénie since she was four, he had no illusions about her character or intelligence and made many sarcastic comments on her elevation to Empress and subsequent career. When she offered him a post as her private secretary, he refused

Jean-Loup Charmet

Roger-Viollet

paddle-steamer from Gravesend to Boulogne via Ramsgate and Rye. The captain, crew and many of the sympathizers he had invited to join him thought they were going on a pleasure cruise. Questions might have been raised in their minds, however, when they spotted a rather scruffy vulture; it had been brought on board to serve as an Imperial Eagle.

The true purpose of the voyage was revealed when they left Rye. The captain was forced to comply with Louis' scheme and the party was ferried ashore near Boulogne by means of a single rowing boat. Unfortunately, the captain in command of the barracks, who, it was hoped, would join the Bonapartist cause, did nothing of the kind.

A shot was fired and a soldier was wounded. Louis Napoleon and his men retreated. Trying to row back to the ship, they were fired on by coastguards and National Guardsmen. In the end, a bedraggled group of revolutionaries were fished out of the water and brought ashore by the French soldiers.

Imprisonment

Louis Philippe was no longer prepared to show clemency: Louis Napoleon was condemned to life imprisonment in the fortress of Ham in Picardy. Imprisoned with him were Conneau and one other member of the expedition, General Montholon. The latter was used to such setbacks – he had already been on St Helena with Napoleon. Louis' valet, Thélin, served a short sentence and then, as a free man, continued to see to his master's needs in prison.

Other needs were attended to by a local girl called Alexandrine Veugeot, who had two sons by Louis during his imprisonment. A beautiful young girl of 20, her day-time employment was doing the ironing for the officers at the fort. When Louis came to power, Alexandrine, like most of his former mistresses, was well provided for financially and the two boys were created Counts under the Empire.

♛ *Louis Philippe* above, *was Duke of Orléans when, at the age of 57, he was elected King of the French by the Chamber of Deputies. He succeeded his cousin, Charles X, last of the Bourbon Kings. Charles had been forced to abdicate in 1830; he had attempted to force a new election because he felt the make-up of the Chamber of Deputies was too liberal*

before she died. Hortense faced pain and death as courageously as she had faced the obstacles encountered in her life. Her chief concern was for the future of her son. She entrusted him to the care of her physician, Dr Conneau.

Returning to England, Louis resumed a life divided between pleasure, plotting and political philosophy. He launched ever more defiant challenges to the regime of the ageing Louis Philippe and published a short work called 'Des Idées Napoliennes'.

Harebrained invasion

In 1840 Louis plunged much of the capital he had inherited from Hortense into a second one-man invasion of France. This time he sailed on a

♛ *Though Louis Napoleon's first one-man invasion of France was treated indulgently by Louis Philippe, his second attempt, in which a soldier was wounded, brought him a life sentence. He was sent to serve it in Picardy, in the medieval Château of Ham* right *where, apart from being confined, he led a more or less normal life*

Roger-Viollet

Louis spent most of the time in serious studies of politics, economics and science, writing on subjects as universal as 'The Extinction of Pauperism' and as parochial as the cultivation of sugar-beet in north-eastern France.

His three rooms — a bedroom, a study and a dining room — were sparsely furnished, damp and badly in need of repair. The damp climate and lack of exercise took a serious toll on his health, but nothing could crush his resilient spirit. After five and a half years, a chance of escape presented itself. The scheme was as ludicrous as his ill-fated expeditions to France, but this time it worked.

Extraordinary escape

While the castle was undergoing repairs, Louis and his fellow-prisoners observed the workmen and the guards to choose the best moment for escape. Early one morning, disguising himself in 'a coarse shirt, a blue blouse and a pair of blue trousers', Louis darkened his face, put on a wig and shaved off his moustache.

While the workmen were distracted by Thélin, who offered them all a drink, Louis picked up a plank and, holding it over his shoulder to conceal his face, strolled across the courtyard and over the drawbridge. At a prearranged spot he was joined by Thélin, who had left the castle on the pretext of taking Louis' dog for a walk.

Meanwhile, Conneau had put a dummy in his bed and told the governor that Louis was ill. With a few minor alarms, Louis and Thélin travelled by cab, post-chaise and train to Belgium and, two days later, the prisoner of Ham

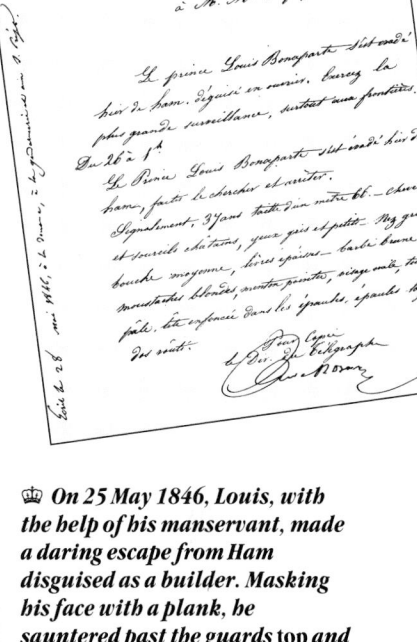

casually booked into a London hotel. The dog, which was also called Ham, made it safely to England, too.

Louis' luck had definitely turned. The Revolution of 1848 was the signal that his time had finally come. In France, Louis Philippe abdicated and a struggle for power ensued between moderate republicans, radicals and socialists. Whatever Louis' political ideas had been in the past, they were no longer in sympathy with any working-class socialist movement. He made this clear in London on 10 April 1848 when, on the occasion of the threatened

On 25 May 1846, Louis, with the help of his manservant, made a daring escape from Ham disguised as a builder. Masking his face with a plank, he sauntered past the guards top *and off to freedom. His absence was not discovered until the next day, and although the prison authorities wrote immediately to the Minister of the Interior above, giving Louis' description and requesting that a look-out be kept at the borders, the fugitive managed to travel via Belgium to a safe haven in England*

RACHEL

Rachel was the stage name of Elisa Félix, the greatest tragic actress of the French classical theatre from the late 1830s until her death in 1858. When the 12-year-old Eugénie was at school in Paris in 1838, she and her sister, Paca, were introduced to Rachel by Mérimée, after they had been delighted by one of her performances. Later, when Eugénie became Empress and was a little unsure of the figure she was presenting, she invited the great Rachel to the Tuileries to coach her in speech and deportment.

Louis Napoleon's path crossed that of Rachel in London in the summer of 1846. He had just escaped from prison in France and she was appearing at the St. James's Theatre in *Phédre*. The great tragedienne *right* was famous for her generosity with her sexual favours, and for a time she consoled Louis during his exile in England

Chartist march on Westminster, he served as one of the 170,000 special constables sworn in for the day.

In June, the barricades went up in Paris and the socialists were slaughtered by the troops of General Cavaignac. The moderates suspected the Bonapartists of having armed the workers, but Napoleon himself was not about to seek power through violent revolution – now he could use the ballot-box, relying on the power and mystique of his name.

President of France

In the by-elections for the National Assembly, held in September, Louis was put up as a candidate for Paris and easily topped the poll. He returned to France to take his seat. Three months later he was standing as candidate for the Presidency of the new Republic. He received 5,434,226 votes, roughly three-quarters of the total cast.

The office of President had little executive power and Louis' term was due to end in 1852. By the Constitution of 1848, he would not be allowed to stand a second time. Leading politi-

Elizabeth Ann Haryet right, universally known as Miss Howard, was 24, and independently wealthy, when she became Louis' mistress in London in 1847. He first established her in a house in Mayfair, then brought her to France in 1848. Louis ended the affair four years later, and made her Countess of Beauregard. She remained in France until her death in 1865

Louis Napoleon was sworn in as President of the French Republic in 1848 below. Though he was officially the Head of State, the President's power was limited by the new constitution. Louis Thiers, leader of the conservative majority party, the Party of Order, considered Louis a womanizer and a fool, and planned to control him by supplying him with mistresses

Roger-Viollet

cians like Louis Adolphe Thiers, who described the Prince-President as a 'cretin', thought Louis would be content with balls, receptions and the company of pretty women, while the real struggle for power was fought out in the National Assembly.

Louis, of course, was as keen as ever on pretty women. After his return to France he arranged for his devoted English mistress, Miss Howard, to follow him. She was installed comfortably in a house not far from the Elysée Palace. Louis made no secret of his attachment, often travelling the country with Miss Howard in his retinue, but his lustful eye continued to rove, seeking new conquests.

A Spanish beauty

At a soirée given by Louis' cousin, Mathilde, in the spring of 1849, his eye lighted for the first time on a young Spanish woman, Eugénie, Countess of Teba. Invitations for Eugénie and her mother had been obtained through the influence of their old friend, Mérimée.

Eugénie had grown into a striking young woman. Mme Carette, who would become one of her ladies-in-waiting, has left a detailed description of her at the time: 'The extremely delicate line of her profile had the perfection of an antique medallion along with something indefinable, a charm all her own, a strange quality that made it impossible to compare her to any other woman.'

As her most striking features, Mme Carette singled out Eugénie's deep blue eyes, her perfect complexion and her tiny feet, 'smaller than those of a 12-year-old child'. It was surprising that such a beauty had not yet become the bride of a Spanish nobleman, but, throughout her teens and early twenties, Eugénie's relations with men had been somewhat capricious.

When Manuela, Paca and Eugénie returned to Spain after Cipriano's death, they lived in Madrid and at their beautiful summer resi-

Edimedia

dence at Carabanchel, not far from the capital. After two years of mourning, Dona Manuela took her place in society again – very much the merry widow. There were fancy-dress balls, visits to the bullfights and amateur theatricals, all of which appealed to Eugénie's sense of drama and romance.

Grand passions

In 1842, Paca became engaged to their cousin, the young Duke of Alba. It was a splendid match, and Eugénie was very happy for Paca. Unfortunately, she was convinced that she too was in love with her cousin and she wrote him a highly emotional letter. It includes such wild statements as, 'You will say that I am romantic and silly, but you are good and will forgive a poor girl who has lost all those that loved her and is now regarded with indifference by everyone, even by her mother, her sister, and, dare I say it, by the man she loves most, for whose sake she would have begged in the street and even consented to her own dishonour.'

'A charm all her own

...that made it impossible

to compare her'

MME CARETTE ON EUGÉNIE

Eugénie was only just 17, so perhaps such outpourings are understandable. She then announces that she will end her days 'in the depths of a sad cloister and no one will ever know that I existed.' Some people have interpreted this letter as a suicide note and linked it with a story that Eugénie once tried to kill herself with phosphorous match-heads swallowed in a glass of milk. However, it was more likely that the suicide attempt, if true, was provoked by a later unrequited passion for Pepe, Marques de Alcañices.

Hard to get

Though Eugénie was capable of conceiving a grand passion for these two men who did not return her love, those who did fall in love with her she treated with scorn or even cruelty. She often seemed bored and dissatisfied and would vent her frustration by making an outrageous spectacle of herself.

On one occasion she performed wild Spanish dances on a billiard table. She clearly liked driving men wild with desire, but was capricious and demanding to such a point that even

Jean-Loup Charmet

her mother despaired of her ever settling down.

When Louis Napoleon learned the identity of the beautiful Spanish girl that he had seen at his cousin's, Eugénie was invited to a reception at the Elysée Palace. This time the Prince-President spoke to her and invited her and her mother to an intimate supper at the Palace of Saint-Cloud.

Any ideas Louis may have entertained of an easy seduction were soon dashed. After the meal, when they went for a walk in the park, Louis tried to take Eugénie's arm. She pointed out that etiquette required him to offer his arm to her mother. Louis conceded the point and escorted Maria Manuela, while Eugénie walked with his chamberlain, Bacciochi. This provocative Spanish girl would not be one of his customary easy conquests.

♛ Louis Napoleon's cousin, Princess Mathilde, kept a fashionable salon at her home in Paris above and acted as hostess at the numerous balls and receptions given by Louis at the Elysée Palace in the early years of his Presidency. It was at one such ball in 1849 that Eugénie and her mother were introduced to Louis for the first time

♛ By 1853 Eugénie left, known universally – and incorrectly – as Mlle de Montijo, had acquired a reputation in Parisian high society not only for her beauty and high spirits but also for her resistance to the blandishments of would-be seducers

Napoleon Museum/Schloss Arenenberg

PALAIS DE COMPIÈGNE

The Palace of Compiègne was one of the three Royal palaces of France capable of holding the entire French court (the others were Versailles and Fontainebleau). The present building dates from the reign of Louis XV, was completed and decorated by Louis XVI and was further redecorated in the Empire style by Napoleon I. Compiègne, however, is principally associated with Napoleon III who made it his official autumn residence and it was here that the Empress Eugénie presided over her famous house parties for the French aristocracy

Lauros-Giraudon

♛ This intricately carved and gilded armoire (cupboard) *above* in Louis XIV style graced the Empress's suite of rooms

☗ Formerly the King's Chamber, this 'family' salon *above* was remodelled in 1855 by Empress Eugénie who simply added more gilding, carving and window decoration to the existing 18th-century decor. The Louis XV-style furniture was actually made in 1859

☗ The Music Room *right* was one of the many rooms redecorated by Empress Eugénie. The red lacquer cabinet is an 18th-century piece of furniture while the gilded armchairs and sofa, once Marie-Antoinette's, were brought from the former Queen's chambers at St Cloud. The comfortable, red upholstered settee and button-back chair date from the 19th century

☗ Compiègne was designed as a summer residence for Louis XV by Ange-Jacques Gabriel. As a result, the facade that overlooks the park *left* is filled with rows of windows to make the interior light and airy

Pictures courtesy of Reunion Musees Nationaux

♛ Huge maps of the Forest of Compiègne line the walls of the Map Room *above*. After dinner, on less formal occasions, guests could retire to this room to play table games or cards if they wished

♛ The Natoire Gallery *below* was constructed in 1858-59. On its walls hang paintings illustrating the life of Don Quixote made by the artist Natoire from 1735 to 1744 as tapestry designs

Réunion Musées Nationaux

Jean-Loup Charmet

♛ Napoleon III, like his uncle, was not above self-promotion. This allegorical painting of himself and the Empress *above* hangs in one of the rooms at Compiègne

♛ The Empress's Bedchamber *right*, with its spectacular bed and gold-embroidered muslin curtains, was originally designed for the Empress Josephine. It shows the First Empire style at its most extravagant

Réunion Musées Nationaux

EMPEROR AND EMPRESS

LOUIS MASTERMINDED A COUP AND BECAME EMPEROR NAPOLEON III. IN SEARCH OF AN EMPRESS, HIS EYE FELL AGAIN ON EUGÉNIE. THEY WERE SOON MARRIED; FRANCE PROSPERED AND AN HEIR TO THE EMPIRE WAS BORN

A FTER THE UNSUCCESSFUL SUPPER AT Saint-Cloud, Louis and Eugénie did not meet again for over a year. During this period Eugénie was courted by several young men, the most persistent being a long-time admirer, the Duke of Osuna. In Brussels, London, Paris and the spa of Eaux-Bonnes in the Pyrenees she was pointed out as 'the Spanish beauty, Mlle de Montijo'.

Over the next two years Louis saw Eugénie at balls or at the Opera when she was in Paris. Although he made no serious overtures, he would give her magnificent bouquets and declare that he had not forgotten her. He had pressing political problems to solve before he could devote himself fully to affairs of the heart.

The men Louis gathered round him at the Elysée included faithful followers from the past like Persigny, along with many new men who had jumped aboard his bandwagon. These included the Duc de Morny, Louis' own half-brother, an illegitimate son of Hortense.

Coup d'état

The political situation of 1851 was as confused as ever; parliamentary democracy created discord rather than order. Louis and Morny decided the time was ripe for a coup d'état. Ostensibly the aim would be to save France from anarchy; in practice it meant guaranteeing Louis power for life.

Although many suspected that Louis was planning a coup of some kind, the conspirators executed 'Operation Rubicon' with chilling

♛ Since he was 20 years old, Louis Napoleon had nursed an ambition to emulate his uncle and become Emperor of France. He took a significant step towards his goal on 2 December 1851 with a decree above which abrogated the National Assembly and made him the supreme power in the land

♛ In the years leading up to the coup d'état, Louis Napoleon left, whose supporters gave him the title Prince-President, was largely preoccupied with his political and social duties. He maintained his liaison with the beautiful Miss Howard, but found his path often crossing that of the bewitching Mlle de Montijo far left

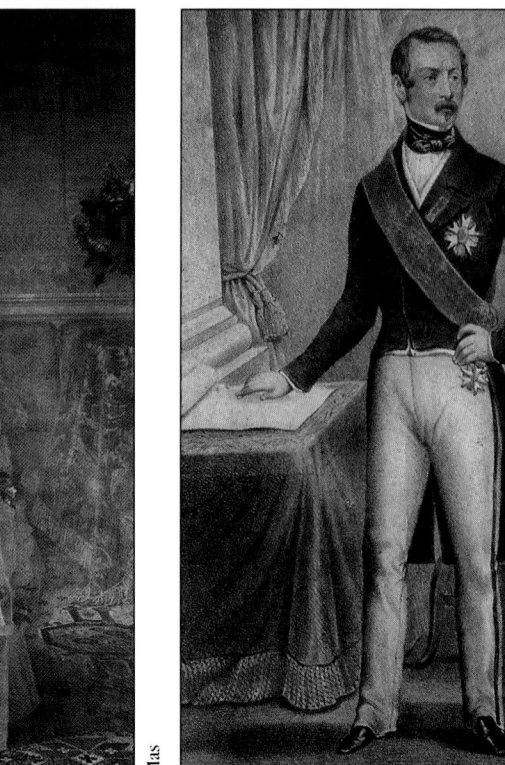

efficiency. On the morning of 2 December 1851, 78 leading deputies, journalists and other political figures woke to find themselves under arrest. The National Assembly and other public buildings were occupied and the streets of Paris were filled with posters proclaiming 'Frenchmen! The present situation cannot continue any longer.'

There was some resistance in the capital, but it was put down ruthlessly on 4 December. Some 400 civilians were killed on the boulevards, many of them innocent bystanders. The blood shed on that day would haunt Louis for the rest of his life. Whenever he was sunk in depression, Eugénie would guess that he was thinking of those days in December 1851. The memory was like 'a bullet that he carried in his foot for twenty years'.

Having seized power with the aid of the military, Louis needed it confirmed by popular vote. In the referendum held on 21 December, 7 ½ million voted in favour of him, with only 650,000 against. The following year the Senate passed a bill establishing the Second Empire. Louis Napoleon became Napoleon III.

In search of a wife

The first concern of a hereditary Emperor is normally to find a wife and produce an heir. At first, Louis intended to make a purely 'political' marriage. A strong candidate was Queen Victoria's niece, Adelaide of Hohenlohe-Langenberg. Negotiations were well advanced when Louis was suddenly diverted from this pragmatic course by the reappearance of the bewitching Eugénie in Paris.

⚜ Louis Napoleon's assumption of the title of Emperor in 1852 met with massive popular support. He symbolized a return to former glories and a certain stability after years of uncertainty and discord. Everywhere he went in the capital he was feted by large crowds above

⚜ Though Louis had certainly been taken with Eugénie's good looks, it was the skill and passion she exhibited in the saddle right, learned as a girl in the long rides through Spain with her father, that finally won his heart. When he saw her flushed with triumph and pleasure after distinguishing herself in a stag hunt at Fontainebleau, he knew he wanted her; less than three months later, they were married

It was in the autumn of 1852, just before the referendum that would confirm the Empire. Louis invited a party of guests to Fontainebleau, including Eugénie and her mother. On Saturday, 13 November there was a hunt. Being a fearless and skilled horsewoman, Eugénie was able to show off all her fire and spirit, riding at the head of the hunt and arriving first at the kill. She was rewarded with the stag's hoof and, following normal convention, rode back to the château with her host.

Mary Evans

Hulton Picture Company

Archiv fur Kunst & Geschichte

Louis was hopelessly smitten. He had never been so consumed by passion. He had once confided to a friend, 'Usually the man attacks; I defend myself and sometimes I yield.' This was different: he had to attack. When they returned to Paris, he sent Eugénie a splendid chestnut horse as a tribute to her skill in the chase.

In December Eugénie and Manuela were invited to join a large party at Compiègne. According to Baron Hübner, the Austrian Ambassador, the Emperor was now 'the victim of a frenzy of passion'. His frenzy reached such a pitch that 'during a ride while he was galloping beside Doña Eugénia, and thinking he was alone ...he addressed to her new and pressing proposals. Mlle de Montijo pulled her horse up short, and looking the Emperor steadily in the eyes, said: "Yes, when I am Empress, yes."'

A similar anecdote has Louis standing beneath her window and asking the way to her room. Eugénie replies, 'Through the chapel, Sire.' Would he really agree to marry her?

Gossip

Once the court realized what was going on, tales such as these and scandalous gossip about Eugénie's past were on everyone's lips. The question that intrigued people was whether Eugénie, who set such store by her virginity, could really be a virgin at the age of 26.

Others were horrified that the Emperor could contemplate marriage with a woman of no consequence. Princess Mathilde is said to have remarked, 'One sleeps with Mlle de Mon-

tijo, one does not marry her.'

Eugénie was in no way 'in love' with her ardent suitor, but she appreciated his good qualities, his calm determination and his willingness to risk everything for love of her. She was also flattered by his chivalrous style of courtship. In a letter to Paca she wrote: 'He would go and look for a flower in the woods on a winter's night ...in order to satisfy the caprice of a woman he loved.'

She was no doubt speaking figuratively, but perhaps was alluding to a famous occasion

'One sleeps with Mlle de Montijo, one does not marry her'

PRINCESS MATHILDE

when she had remarked on the beauty of a clover leaf covered in dew. Immediately Louis had a fabulous emerald and diamond brooch made up in the shape she admired.

The Emperor, meanwhile, had all but forgotten the possibility of a marriage with Adelaide. Luckily, news came that she had refused his offer. This was after he had already decided to marry Eugénie – there might have been a very nasty diplomatic incident.

On 15 January 1853, Louis at last sent a formal proposal of marriage to Maria Manuela: 'Madame la Comtesse. For a long time I have loved Mademoiselle your daughter and wished to make her my wife. Today, therefore, I am asking for her hand, because no one is more capable than she of making me

♛ *The nuptial mass of Emperor Louis Napoleon and Eugénie in Notre Dame in 1853* top left *was a glittering, if hastily arranged, occasion. It was the first wedding of a reigning monarch in France since Louis XV in 1725. The couple* above *travelled to and from the cathedral in the coach* top right *that had been used half a century before to take Napoleon and Josephine to the ceremony at which they were crowned Emperor and Empress*

♛ *Soon after her wedding, the new Empress sat for her first official portrait* right, *which captured her pale colouring and the slightly melancholy expression that her face habitually took on in repose*

HAUSSMANN'S PARIS

Although the Second Empire lasted less than 20 years, the public works carried out under Napoleon III have had a lasting effect. The Paris we know today was largely created by Georges Eugène Haussmann, appointed Prefect of the Department of the Seine in 1853. Vast areas of old housing were swept away, with the Emperor's approval *right* in order to drive a series of wide new boulevards through the city. This eased the circulation of traffic and did much to improve the health of the overcrowed city, but was extremely unpopular at the time.

Other innovations accepted more readily by the Parisians included new railway stations, a new central market at Les Halles and the landscaping of the Bois de Boulogne, making it one of the finest public parks in the world. The Bois was linked to the city by the 'Avenue de l'Impératrice', but at the fall of the Empire all the street-names glorifying Napoleon and Eugénie were changed

Jean-Loup Charmet

happy or more worthy to wear a crown.'

Once the engagement became public knowledge, the Emperor decided they should marry as soon as possible. Gossip about Eugénie proliferated and details from her mother's colourful life were also coming to light. An early wedding might put an end to all this muck-raking. The civil ceremony was therefore arranged for 29 January with a nuptial mass in Notre Dame on the following day.

Wedding day

The gloomy interior of the cathedral was hastily transformed with flags and brightly-coloured hangings, gilt crowns and the initials 'L' and 'E'. Many people complained that the effect was too gaudy, but few Royal weddings can have been organized at such short notice. Eugénie's sister and brother-in-law did not even have time to make the trip from Madrid.

The civil ceremony on the Saturday evening was a frightening ordeal for Eugénie. It took place at the Tuileries and was attended by several members of the Bonaparte family who barely acknowledged her presence. King Jerome and his son, Prince Napoleon, were the worst offenders. She had to sit on a throne for three-quarters of an hour, while diplomats and ministers filed by. 'I was paler than the jasmine that I wore on my heart,' she wrote to Paca. She and her mother slept at the Elysée, while Louis remained at the Tuileries. They were not yet married in the eyes of God.

Eugénie was still pale the next morning as

Bridgeman

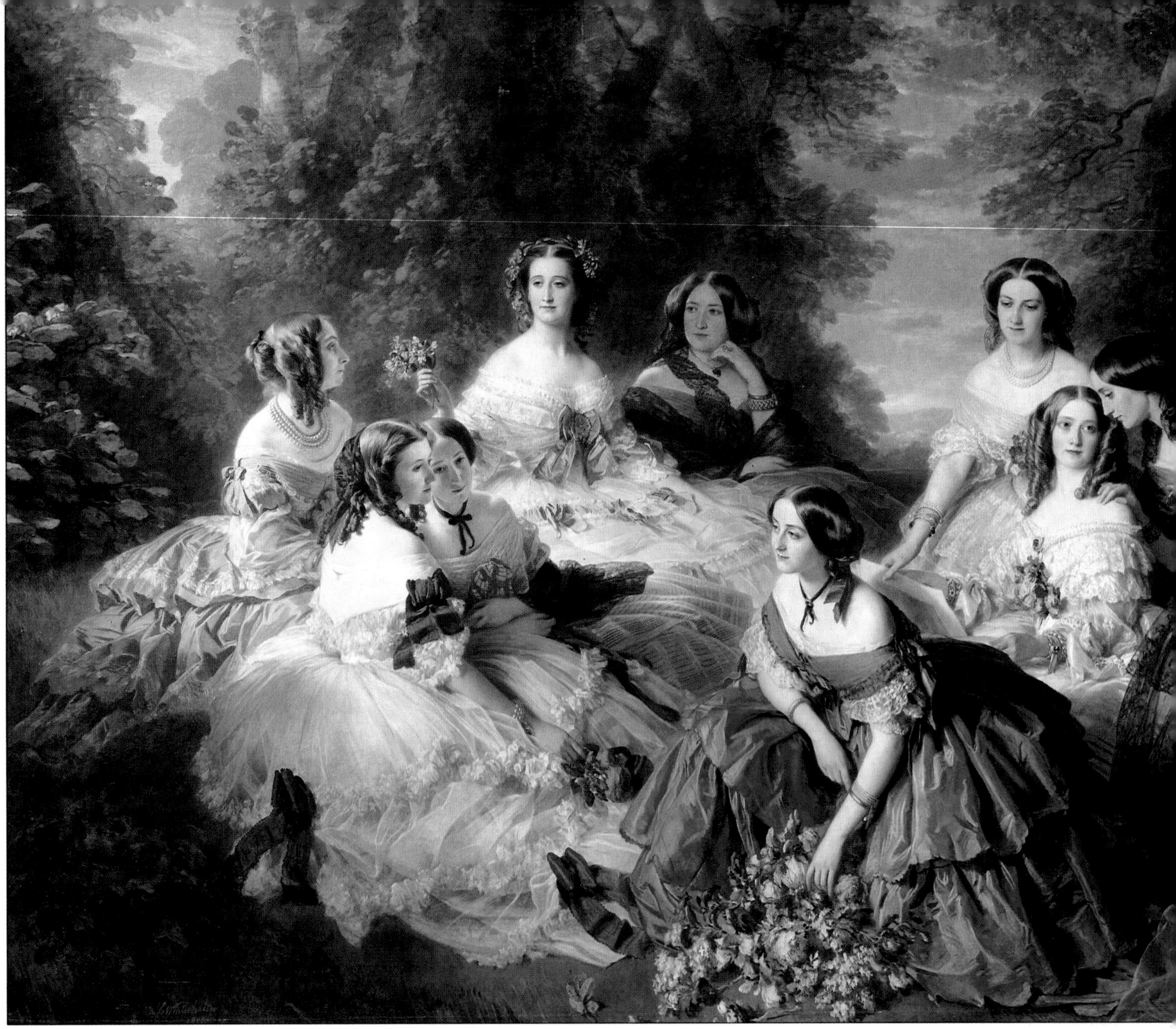

Lauros-Giraudon

BIARRITZ

The Empress would always spend late summer and early autumn at the Villa Eugénie in Biarritz, on France's south-west coast *right*. She and Napoleon had visited the small town in 1854, the year after their marriage, and by the following year the new villa was almost complete. Dr Barthez, the physician to the Prince Imperial, described it as 'a little château, a mere chocolate-box, built of brick and stone, with one storey above ground floor.' However, its spacious lawns, guardrooms and private chapel set it apart from the other seaside homes that soon started to spring up once Biarritz became a fashionable resort.

Eugénie's love of Biarritz lay in the fact that it was in the Basque country, close to Spain. Trips by steamer to San Sebastian were sometimes organized for the guests. The Villa Eugénie did not outlive its mistress – the building was destroyed in a fire in 1903

Jean-Loup Charmet

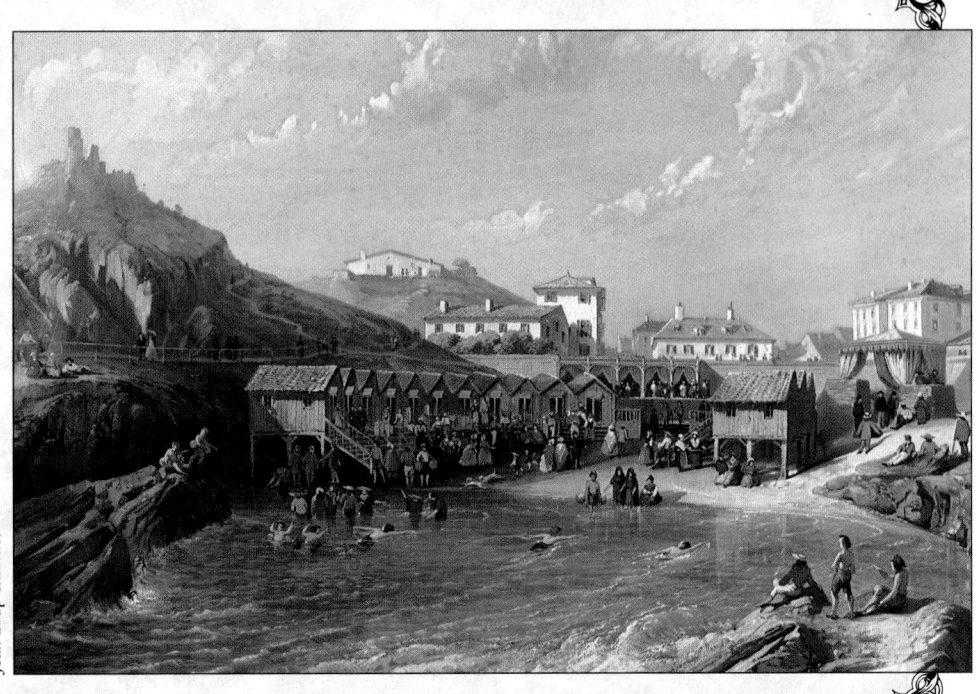

the wedding procession drove down the newly-completed Rue de Rivoli. The couple rode in a coach that had been used for the coronation of Napoleon and Joséphine in 1804. Thousands of curious sight-seers flocked to Paris to catch a glimpse of their new Empress.

She wore a dress of white satin with a train four metres long. The bodice was sewn with diamonds and finished by a diamond-encrusted belt. Over the whole was draped a shawl of old lace. Her veil was also of priceless antique lace and her hari was trimmed with orange blossom. As a crown, she wore a magnificent diadem that had belonged to Joséphine.

⚜ Eugénie was painted several times by the great Court painter, Franz Xaver Winterhalter, at the beginning of her reign. In 1854 below she posed in classic style. The following year she was shown left among her ladies-in-waiting, wearing a white dress trimmed with lilac silk

Roger-Viollet

Louis Napoleon in his general's uniform looked proud and happy, but it was not the Emperor people had come to see. The day was a triumph for Eugénie. She won the hearts of all who managed to catch sight of her.

Wedded bliss

For the first few months of marriage there was nothing to cloud their happiness. Miss Howard had been bought off a with a fine country house and the title of Countess. Maria Manuela, who could have proved an embarrassment, returned to Spain to live with her other daughter, Paca. Louis and Eugénie spent as much time as they could together; palace officials and visitors to the Tuileries were liable, on entering a room, to find the Empress sitting on the Emperor's knee.

Lord Cowley, the British Ambassador, reported back to Whitehall: 'The Emperor thinks of nothing but his beautiful Empress to the neglect of all business.' Eugénie was determined to produce an heir for her attentive husband. Cowley's comment on the matter of children

'The Emperor thinks of nothing but his beautiful Empress'

BRITISH AMBASSADOR

was: 'Napoleon will want one, as he wants everything, in haste ...before the time laid down by the laws of nature.'

As it turned out, nature played a cruel trick on the Imperial couple – at the end of April, Eugénie suffered a miscarriage. Louis did everything he could to console Eugénie, showing only concern for her health and no disappointment at the loss of the child.

Sexual problems

There is no doubt that from the very first there were problems in the Imperial bedchamber. Louis was 44 and accustomed to the instant gratification of his sexual desires; Eugénie's opinion of physical love was, 'Isn't it disgusting!' Louis later said that it was only six months after the wedding that he started to indulge in 'little amusements' once again.

At times, Eugénie found this impossible to tolerate and there were angry scenes between them. One thing Louis could not stand was a domestic row and she learned to get her own way just by threatening to make a scene. But she could never put a stop to his infidelities.

LEADER OF FASHION

In public, on the other hand, Eugénie surpassed everybody's expectations, even her husband's. Her slightly sad beauty and relatively humble origins made her a subject of fascination throughout Europe. The panache with which she wore her crinoline dresses from Mlle Palmyre made her the leader of Paris fashion.

As a schoolgirl she had been teased on account of her hair; now women copied her style of wearing it – pulled back austerely from a central parting with a shower of ringlets at the nape of the neck. Many even dyed their hair red in imitation of their beautiful Empress.

♛ In April 1855, Emperor Napoleon III received a token of his acceptance into the Royal Houses of Europe when, on a State visit to Britain to mark the two nations' cooperation in the Crimean War, he was invested with the Order of the Garter by Queen Victoria in a ceremony at Windsor Castle above

♛ Later in 1855, the British Royal Family made a reciprocal State visit to France for the opening of the Exposition Universelle, whose buildings, including a Palace of Industry below celebrated the achievements of the new Empire

Louis' first aim for his Empire was to encourage economic growth. France needed to catch up with England in the building of steamships, railways and telegraphs. Schemes were financed by a mixture of private capital and government funds. Speculators on the Bourse, like Louis' half-brother, Morny, made and lost fabulous fortunes. Nevertheless, Louis' economic policy was successful – France did become more prosperous.

Amidst the red plush, gilt and crystal chandeliers that characterized the prosperity of the Second Empire, the figure of Eugénie, dressed in Alençon lace and silks from Lyons, completed the picture to perfection. Implacable critics of the regime, like the exiled Victor Hugo, maintained that all this luxury was an illusion that would ultimately shatter.

In his foreign policy, Louis' aim was to restore France's prestige in Europe. The first opportunity came with the Crimean War, in which France and England found themselves allied against Russia in support of Turkey. Friendly relations with England called for an exchange of visits with Queen Victoria and Prince Albert.

Charming the English
In 1854, Napoleon and Albert had a preliminary meeting at Boulogne, where the Emperor was reviewing his troops. Having heard all about Louis' loose morals, Albert was not disposed to like him, but he found his host 'quiet and indolent from constitution, not easily excited, but gay and humorous at his ease.' He objected to his incessant smoking, however.

In April 1855 a state visit to London and Windsor was arranged. Eugénie and Victoria, who thought her guest 'tactful, yet natural in her manner', discovered they had much to talk about. 'She is deeply touched by my affection

and care for her,' wrote Victoria in a letter. 'She is, alas, not at all strong.' This was a reference to Eugénie's lack of success in bearing children. Eugénie had had a second miscarriage the previous year and had needed a long holiday in Biarritz to recuperate.

More surprisingly, Victoria also took to Louis Napoleon. She was impressed by his 'unflinching firmness of purpose' and his 'self-control', but he also had a 'power of fascination'. Victoria was completely won over by his quiet charm and gentle humour. After she had invested him with the Order of the Garter at a ball at Windsor Castle, he whispered to her, 'Enfin, je suis gentilhomme.'

Later that year the visit was returned. Paris was holding its first 'Exposition Universelle', in imitation of London's Great Exhibition of 1851. Albert marvelled not only at the exhibition itself, but also at all the new roads and restored buildings in Paris: 'How all this could have been done in so short a time no one comprehends.'

Before the visit Eugénie had discovered she was pregnant again and had been advised to take things easy. When she was with the Royal party, things were not as friendly as before, but in private Victoria gave her lots of sound, sisterly advice on gynaecological matters and antenatal care.

Bridgeman

A son and heir

How much of Victoria's advice Eugénie followed we do not know, but the following March Queen Victoria felt almost personally responsible for the safe delivery into the world of the Prince Imperial.

The birth of a son, the event for which Eugénie had prayed for so long, coincided with the high point of Louis' political fortunes. The Crimean War was over and the Peace Congress in Paris was confirming that France now had the most powerful voice in European affairs.

The Congress was adjourned when the Empress went into labour. At one point when the situation looked critical, Louis was asked whether the mother or the child should be saved. Louis replied, 'The mother'. Fortunately it proved to be a false alarm and, after 22 hours, Eugénie gave birth to a large, healthy boy. Louis, who throughout the birth had been the archetype of a nervous, chain-smoking father-to-be, rushed into the anteroom and embraced the first five people he met.

☖ *During their visit to France, Victoria and Albert stayed with the imperial couple at their official residence, the Palais de Compiègne, just outside Paris. Away from their official duties, Victoria and the pregnant Eugénie spent some time together, riding in the château's extensive grounds above and huge forest*

Jean-Loup Charmet

☖ *The birth of the Prince Imperial, the only baby Eugénie ever managed to carry to term, in 1856 filled the Emperor with pride left. He was at the zenith of his career; he had assured the succession, and the victory of the allied armies over the Russians in the Crimea had re-established France as the great military power on mainland Europe*

Dress bodice of white velvet

♛ Eugénie photographed in London in the 1870s. Her plain silk gown has a fichu of white lace held in place by a contrasting rosette. An antique cameo is her only jewellery

♛ The antique lace for Eugénie's wedding gown was valued at 40,000 francs. She wore two Napoleonic heirlooms; one, around her waist, was a circlet of sapphires and diamonds given by Napoleon I to Empress Marie-Louise

♛ In her stylish bonnet and day dress, Eugénie was as elegant as in her formal Court-dress portraits by Winterhalter

Wedding gown features Alençon lace veil, tiered skirt and sleeve trim

ARBITER OF TASTE

All her contemporaries agree that the Empress Eugénie had that rare gift of exquisite taste in dress. It was she who encouraged and, indeed, made the fortunes of the couturier, Charles Frederick Worth, by bestowing her patronage on him. The essential feminity and relative simplicity of his gowns appealed to her and he in turn responded by creating masterpieces of elegance for her

♛ Eugénie chose this Worth-designed gown of red velvet trimmed with sable for one of the portraits painted of her (with the Prince Imperial) by her favourite artist, Winterhalter

Full crinoline velvet skirt

Bodice with shaped basque trimmed with fur

TRIUMPHS AND FOLLIES

WITH EUGÉNIE UNABLE TO HAVE MORE CHILDREN, LOUIS SOUGHT SOLACE WITH HIS MISTRESSES. FRANCE TASTED MILITARY SUCCESS IN ITALY BUT OTHER VENTURES FAILED AND LOUIS' HEALTH BEGAN TO DECLINE

❦ Eugénie became a favourite subject of Winterhalter, who never failed to capture her wistful beauty below. His portraits of Napoleon III are more formal. In 1857 he painted him looking dignified and inscrutable behind his waxed moustachios right and wearing his characteristic dress of an English-tailored black frock coat with the rosette of the Legion d'Honneur in his buttonhole

AT THE BEGINNING OF THIS CENTURY, Eugénie, by then an old lady, was asked by a writer which were the most splendid moments of her reign. Without hesitation, she replied, 'First and foremost, the christening of the Prince Imperial'. It had taken Eugénie a long time to recover from the difficult birth, and the ceremonial christening was delayed until June. She was becoming increasingly devout, so was delighted that the Pope agreed to be godfather – by proxy. The baby, who howled lustily throughout the ceremony, was given the names Napoleon Eugène Louis Jean Joseph.

When they were at home together, the

Giraudon

Napoleon Museum Schloss Arenenberg

Emperor and Empress vied with each other in their doting concern for their son. Loulou, as his father usually called him, became the focal point of their life; without him their marriage might never have survived.

After the birth, Eugénie had been told she would be risking her life if she ever tried to have another child. This was in some ways a relief to her, but it meant that her husband's infidelities became more frequent.

He continued to treat his wife kindly, he still teased her gently and called her by his pet name for her, 'Oogenie', but for physical satisfaction he looked elsewhere.

Mistresses

One beauty Louis had fallen for – even before the birth of the Prince Imperial – was Virginie, Countess di Castiglione. She had in fact been

Roger-Viollet

♛ *The Emperor had not been married long before his eye began once again to rove. One of the first court beauties upon which it lighted was Virginie, Countess of Castiglione, in northern Italy* top. *She was supplanted in his affections by Marianne, Countess Walewska* above, *the wife of one of his ministers*

♛ *The attempt on the Imperial couple's life by Italian revolutionaries Orsini, Rudio, Gomez and Pieri* right *brought down the government of Britain, whence the conspirators had come, and led to repressive measures in France. Orsini's patriotism and dignity so impressed Louis and Eugénie that they sought his reprieve, but he and Pieri were executed, and their accomplices jailed*

sent by Cavour, the Prime Minister of Piedmont, with express instructions to seduce the Emperor, find out his feelings on the subjects of Italian unification and to try to influence his foreign policy.

As a spy she proved useless, for, by all accounts, she hadn't a brain in her head, but her talent as a seductress was undeniable. Eugénie could not stand la Castiglione — she always seemed especially distressed when Louis slept with women she felt were beneath him.

In contrast to la Castiglione, who flaunted her liaison with the Emperor outrageously, his next mistress was not only discretion itself, she even became a close friend of Eugénie and a member of her intimate circle of ladies at the Court. This was Marianne Walewska, the wife of Louis' foreign minister. On one occasion, while travelling on the Imperial train to Compiègne, Princess Mathilde saw her cousin Louis sitting 'à cheval' on Marianne's knee, 'kissing her on the mouth and plunging his hand down her bosom'.

Fortunately, Eugénie never had to witness such scenes, but her husband's 'distractions' caused her enormous suffering. In a mood of black despair, she wrote to Paca; 'I have such a disgust of life — it is so empty as to the past, so full of pitfalls in the present and perhaps so short for the future — at least I hope so — that I often wonder if it is worth the trouble of struggling.' She never lost the flair for the melodramatic she had exhibited as a young girl.

Bomb outrage

Her premonition that she might not have long to live almost proved to be true. On 14 January 1858, just as Napoleon and Eugénie drew up in their carriage outside the Opéra, a group of Italian conspirators, led by a man called Orsini, threw three bombs. The street was packed with opera-goers, onlookers and a large cavalry escort. More than 150 people were wounded and eight were killed, but the Emperor and Empress, apart from a few cuts from flying glass, were unharmed.

AISA

Louis wanted to stay and talk to the wounded, but Eugénie hurried him inside — there might have been a fourth bomb. The orchestra struck up *'Partant pour la Syrie'*, the tune composed by Louis' mother, Hortense, and the gala performance went ahead as planned.

It was at moments like this that the French rallied to their Emperor and Empress with spontaneous feelings of uncritical affection. There were other attempts on the Emperor's life — by radicals and socialists as well as Italian patriots — but Orsini's was the one that came closest to success.

Italian battles

Louis had always wanted to do something to unify Italy, which was split into eight states. Eugénie, supported by an increasingly powerful Catholic party in France, would not hear of Louis supporting revolution against the Papal States — after all, the Pope was godfather of their son. In the end, Louis sent a French army to Lombardy, to oust the ruling Austrians.

In 1859, at Magenta and Solferino, Napoleon took his place as commander-in-chief on the field of battle. Although he showed no fear for his personal safety, he had little stomach for the carnage he witnessed. He did nothing to rival the deeds of his uncle, Napoleon I. Indeed, he spent most of the time nervously smoking. Modern weapons had changed the nature of warfare; the battles were won, but at enormous cost. It was the terrible scene after Solferino, with the wounded left to die where they lay,

that prompted the Geneva Convention of 1864 and the setting up of the International Red Cross by a Swiss philanthropist.

Acting as Regent

The war in Italy had an important consequence at home. In the absence of the Emperor, Eugénie was named Regent and presided over the regular Councils of Ministers. She needed courage to argue with men like Jerome's son, Prince Napoleon, whose policy on Italy was totally opposed to hers, but she relished the chance to get back at critics who called her 'frivolous, extravagant, coquettish, giddy'.

When the victory at Solferino was celebrated in July with a solemn Te Deum at Notre Dame, Eugénie felt a glow of personal satisfaction. The Prince Imperial travelled with her in the carriage; he was 'quivering with joy, clap-

⚜ Italian independence was a popular cause in France, and Louis' decision to lead the French troops in battle against the Austrians who were occupying Lombardy had the support of the vast majority of the people, who thronged the streets of the capital to wish him well above

⚜ The Italian adventure was no less popular with the young Prince Imperial, portrayed here with his father right, *who 'quivered with joy' on his way to the victory celebrations at Notre Dame cathedral*

⚜ The battle of Solferino left, *where the French under Napoleon fought alongside the Piedmontese under Victor Emmanuel against Emperor Franz Josef's Austrians, was the last time three reigning sovereigns appeared on the same battlefield. The extraordinary carnage made it rather a Pyrrhic victory for the French. A total of 40,000 men on all sides were lost; many of the wounded lay unattended for three days*

⚜ After good relations were restored, Richard Metternich was appointed Austrian ambassador to France. The straightforward, serious-minded Richard and his mischievous, fun-loving wife, Pauline, right *became Eugénie's best friends at court*

Jean-Loup Charmet

Reunion Musees Nationaux

Roger-Viollet

ping his hands and throwing the prettiest kisses to the crowds ...I had the dazzling certainty that God was reserving for my child the glorious mission of crowning his father's work.' She, too, had found a mission in life; 'Nothing used to irritate me more than to hear myself denied a political sense because I was a woman.'

Eugénie's close friends

Eugénie's greatest friends throughout the last ten years of the Empire were Richard and Pauline Metternich, the Austrian Ambassador

> ## 'Clapping his hands and throwing the prettiest kisses to the crowds'

THE YOUNG PRINCE IMPERIAL

and his wife. Richard was the son of the great statesman who had restored the stability of Europe after Waterloo. While Eugénie discussed serious politics with Richard, she kept alive her youthful sense of fun with Pauline.

Pauline was fond of singing 'little Parisian songs, which are frivolous and broad – very broad'. During parties at Biarritz, Pauline, Eugénie and her ladies would roll up napkins and rush around trying to hit the gentlemen.

MAISON WORTH

In 1846 a penniless young Englishman, named Charles Frederick Worth, sailed to France hoping to make his fortune in the world of fashion.

In 1860 Pauline Metternich, Eugénie's unconventional friend, wore a Worth creation to a great ball at the Tuileries. In her *Souvenirs* she recalls that 'The Empress immediately saw it was a chef-d'oeuvre. She came up to me and at once asked who had made this wonderfully pretty dress, so simple and yet so elegant ...Worth was launched, I was lost, for from then on I knew there would be no more gowns for me at 300 francs.' Eugénie, portrayed here in a Worth dress *right*, became one of his best customers.

Simplicity was what distinguished Worth's designs from the monstrous creations of the age of the crinoline. A Worth fashion that was particularly associated with the Empress, from about 1863, was the ankle-length walking dress

Jean-Loup Charmet

Pauline and Eugénie were also said to have dressed up as men and ridden around Paris on top of a horse-drawn omnibus. Eugénie may have been a prude when it came to action, but she loved Pauline's risqué songs and stories and her outspoken comments on the people she met at court.

Louis was sometimes embarrassed by the freedom with which Eugénie expressed herself. There were cultural differences between them that were never really bridged. She loved

⚜ *Following the victories in Italy, Napoleon III's popularity approached its zenith. He was considered one of the great rulers of Europe. A painting put him at the centre of a group of monarchs comprising* above, left to right *King Oscar of Sweden, King William of Prussia, Emperor Franz Josef, Napoleon, the Tsar of Russia, the Shah of Persia and King Leopold of Belgium*

'The wedding, for all time, of France and the Empire'

EUGÉNIE IN SAVOY

talking and he preferred to remain silent, weighing up the situation before committing himself. His silence when Eugénie's sister died and he thought it would be better not to tell her was to cause a serious rift between them.

Triumphal tour

In 1860 they went on an extended tour together, visiting Savoy and Nice, the territories France had gained after the war in Italy, then Corsica, to visit the cradle of the Bonaparte

⚜ *Like her husband, Eugénie, too, took on a more regal air with the passing years. Painted in 1862 by Winterhalter* right, *enthroned and cloaked in ermine, she appeared every inch the Empress*

Mas

family, and finally the French colony of Algeria. Paca, who was seriously ill, had come to Paris with her mother and her children. Eugénie had left, thinking her sister was making good progress. She wrote to her regularly from the places they visited; the letters were full of the enthusiastic receptions she and Louis received on their travels.

Eugénie was enjoying herself hugely. At Annecy in Savoy there was a spectacular regatta on the lake. Standing on the deck of a gondola, with cries of 'Vive l'Impératrice' ringing in her ears, she imagined herself as 'present at the wedding, for all time, of France and the Empire.' The reception she received in Algeria was just as warm.

A rift

Louis was glad to see her so radiantly happy, so when he received the sad news of Paca's death, he kept it from her until they were about to land again in France. Eugénie was furious that he had not told her immediately. She also gave vent to all her pent-up feelings about his affairs and blamed him for his failure to support Papal troops in Italy. Napoleon was astonished at the vehemence of her attack.

Once Paca's body had been despatched to Madrid, Eugénie announced that she was going away for a while – alone. She decided to visit England and Scotland, travelling incognita as the Comtesse de Pierrefonds, accompanied by

♛ *Eugénie remained close to her sister Paca* right, *who grew to resemble her more and more as they got older. When Louis waited five days before giving her the news of Paca's death – from a rare spine disease following cancer of the breast – she was inconsolable, and rounded on her husband*

♛ *Louis and Eugénie were soon reconciled, and were always sure to present a united front when they appeared in public or promenaded through the grounds of Compiègne with the Prince Imperial* below

just two ladies and two gentlemen. She suspected she might be suffering from the disease that had killed Paca and wanted to consult a doctor in Edinburgh. When she returned to France, after an absence of a month, Louis went to meet her at Amiens.

ERRORS OF JUDGEMENT

Louis, in the meantime, had given way to his wife in one matter: he had sent French troops to Rome. At Eugénie's insistence, Louis also embarked on a futile attempt to establish Maximilian, the brother of the Emperor of Austria, as Emperor of Mexico. Louis sent French troops to Mexico to bolster the new Empire, but in 1866, under pressure from the United States, he was forced to withdrawn them. A year later, Maximilian surrendered to the republican forces of Juarez and was executed by firing squad.

The event that signalled the demise of the Second Empire was not the failure of Napoleon's own enterprises, but the emergence of Prussia as a threatening military power. In 1866, Prussia totally defeated the Austrians in a war that lasted only seven weeks. Louis Napoleon might have acted to prevent Prussia from annexing the North German states, but he was now a sick man and was no match for the cunning diplomacy of Bismarck.

At home, too, Louis was losing his grip on affairs. His advisers were split, some favouring the autocratic form of government he had once employed, others pressing for greater liberalization. Eugénie, who had enjoyed a second period as Regent, was now insisting on attend-

ing regularly at his councils. This made decision-making even more difficult.

His wife and doctors were worried about Louis' greyish complexion and his dragging gait, but at this point they do not seem to have diagnosed the real trouble – an enormous stone in his bladder.

But a man like Louis would never let ill-health stop him from doing what he saw as his duty. He had to keep the Empire alive for his

🔖 *The Exposition Universelle was in many ways the Last Hurrah of the Second Empire. Visitors flocked from all over Europe to see not only the exhibits but the contrast between the glass and metal buildings and the relatively informal gardens* above

EXPOSITION UNIVERSELLE, 1867

The 'Exposition Universelle', held in Paris in 1867, was the largest and most expensive international trade fair of its time, with total exhibition space of over 6,000,000 sq ft. The main exhibits, which included everything from Japanese clothes to a monstrous cannon from the Krupp steelworks, were housed in a vast palace of glass and iron that was erected on the Champ de Mars *right*. Even before it was opened on 1 April, 5,000 visitors a day flocked to the site simply to watch the preparations.

In June, the Tsar of Russia, the King of Prussia, the Sultan of Turkey and the brother of the Mikado joined the thousands flocking to the exhibition. One of the most popular attractions was a park containing examples of modern buildings, ranging from a Turkish mosque to an English lighthouse. There were also, for the first time at any such exhibition, cafés and restaurants serving food and drink from around the world

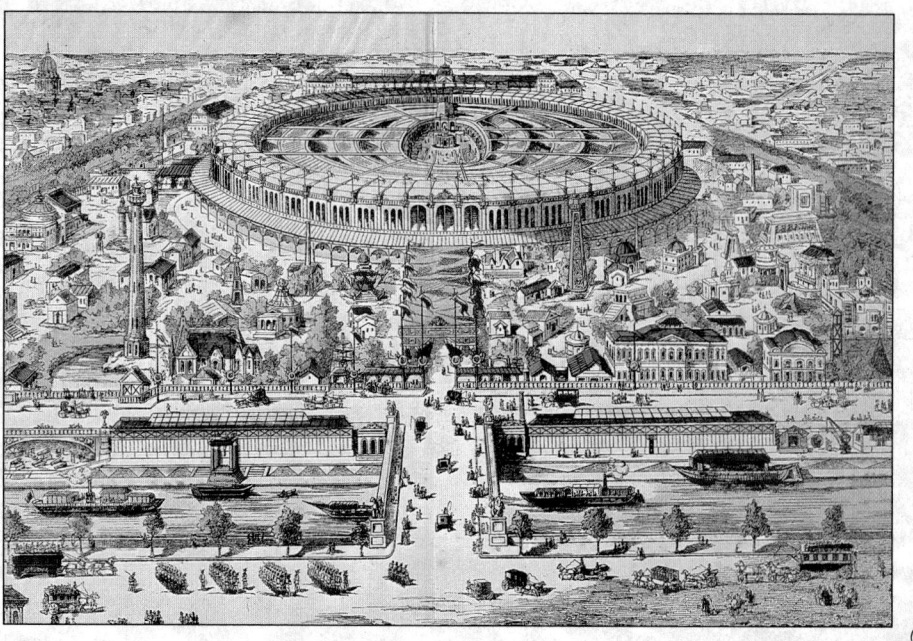

Roger-Viollet

♛ *Louis dressed as a Guardsman*

Roger-Viollet

♛ *Napoleon and Louis prepare for a drive*

Mary Evans

♛ *The youthful Prince in military uniform*

Mansell Collection

♛ *A formal portrait of Eugénie,*
Napoleon and the Prince Imperial

LOST HORIZONS

The imperial dreams of Napoleon III and Eugénie were shattered but not totally lost by defeat and exile in 1870. For the beautiful and brave Eugénie, hope lay not so much in her beloved but ailing husband but in their handsome young son; he was tragically killed six years after the death of his father, leaving Eugénie alone with 20 more years of sad and happy memories

👑 The scene outside Notre Dame on the day of the Royal wedding in 1853 was captured by a photographer *above right*. Louis and Eugénie's beloved son was born in 1856. Aged two, the Prince Imperial poses on a pony for the photographer, watched over by his father and a groom *above*

👑 Eugénie would have specially treasured this picture of her husband gazing fondly on their young son *right*. In them, she had invested all her own ambitions, dreams and hopes for the future, and at the time of this photograph there was every chance of their fulfilment

👑 The official visit of the Emperor and Empress to Britain in 1855 *right* was a particularly happy occasion. Eugénie especially remembered the gallantry of Prince Albert towards her and the kindness of Queen Victoria. As a country of exile many years later, England was therefore not only a safe place but a welcome refuge among old friends

👑 Napoleon III *above*, as Eugénie liked to remember him — cultured, urbane and kindly. 'When I am free,' he wrote to her from prison, 'I should like to go to England and live with you and Louis in a little cottage with bow-windows and a creeper.' Camden Place, Chislehurst *right*, where Napoleon spent the last years of his life, was in fact a large country house full of servants

Mary Evans

A FALSE STEP!
THE ROAD TO RUIN.

HUMILIATION AND EXILE

WAR WITH PRUSSIA WAS TO DESTROY THE SECOND EMPIRE. EUGÉNIE AND THE PRINCE IMPERIAL FLED TO ENGLAND, LATER TO BE JOINED BY LOUIS. FOR EUGÉNIE IT WAS TO BE A LONG EXILE

☖ *As the political realities of Europe changed, so Napoleon III's Empire became increasingly vulnerable. The cartoon above, published in 1868, foresaw war with Prussia in 1869, and a final reckoning with England in 1870*

☖ *Eugénie at her favourite retreat, Biarritz below. She and Napoleon were there on holiday in 1868 when the Spanish queen, Isabella, was deposed*

T OWARDS THE END OF HIS REIGN, NAPOLEON was suffering increasing agony from the stone in his bladder. He had great difficulty in concentrating on affairs of state and allowed the opposition liberties they would never have got away with before.

The journalist, Henri Rochefort, published satirical articles such as his famous assessment of the House of Bonaparte. He declared that his favourite was Napoleon II. 'No one can deny that he occupied the throne, for his successor is called Napoleon III. What a reign, my friends, what a reign! No taxes, no futile wars followed by war levies, no distant expeditions costing six hundred million francs to get back fifteen …Yes, Napoleon II, I love and admire you with all my heart!'

Eugénie was to remember Rochefort's attacks with bitterness for the rest of her life, especially those that mocked her political pretensions. She now took herself very seriously as Empress, knowing that Napoleon could die, leaving her as Regent for the Prince Imperial.

Ominous events
In the autumn of 1868, when Napoleon and Eugénie were on holiday at Biarritz, they received an unscheduled visit from Queen Isabella of Spain, who had been forced to flee her country. The upshot of the revolution was that Spain needed another monarch and the new government went looking for one among the Royal Houses of Europe.

The candidate who emerged was Prince Leopold Hohenzollern, a member of the Prussian ruling House. France could never tolerate a Hohenzollern on the throne of Spain and so began the battle of words that, through the skilful management of Bismarck, would inflame French anger against Prussia until they were forced to go to war. When the Imperial party left Biarritz that year, it was the last holiday they would ever take at the Villa Eugénie.

Magnificent spectacle
In 1869, the reason they did not go to Biarritz was that Eugénie had been invited to open the Suez Canal. She took her nieces, Paca's two daughters, with her and enjoyed the chance to escape from the hostility of Rochefort and his fellow journalists. Describing the opening of the canal, which had been engineered by Ferdinand de Lesseps, a distant relative, she recalled: 'The spectacle was so supremely magnificent, and proclaimed so proudly the greatness of the French regime, that I could contain myself no longer: I was exultant.'

Roger-Viollet

The French regime, meanwhile, was on its last legs. Scandals about the speculation that had gone on in the redevelopment of Paris in the 1850s had tarnished the reputations of many of Napoleon's closest advisers. Louis spent the time Eugénie was away in organizing a new Liberal government to be headed by one of his former opponents in the National Assembly, Emile Ollivier.

Eugénie felt betrayed; she had tried to influence her husband from far away in Egypt, writing to him that, 'Continuity of policy is the only real strength. I dislike violent changes, and I do not believe that it is possible to bring off a coup d'état twice in one reign.'

The Ollivier Government, which became known as the 'Ministry of Good Intentions', eventually took office in January 1870. Its good intentions were never seriously put to the test. The war that Bismarck had been engineering since 1866 put all thought of domestic policy out of the public mind.

In July anti-Prussian feeling was so strong that people of every political persuasion were demonstrating together in the streets of Paris. The Empress was almost fanatical in her support for the war; she thought a victory would make the throne finally safe for her son to inherit. The Emperor, old and weak, was not so sure she was right.

War with Prussia

War was declared on 15 July 1870. At the end of the month, Napoleon, too weak to ride a horse, set off by train to take command of his troops at Metz. With him he took the 14-year-old Prince Imperial, who was thrilled to be wearing the uniform of a second lieutenant and to be carrying a sword. He had little idea of the reality of the situation.

Neither did his father – instead of the 385,000 troops he had expected to find at the

Eugénie took the opportunity offered by the opening of the Suez Canal to travel through Egypt, a land whose destiny was interwoven with that of the Napoleons through the 19th century, visiting the Pyramids and other relics from the time of the Pharaohs above

'The spectacle was so supremely magnificent'

EUGÉNIE ON THE SUEZ CANAL

THE SUEZ CANAL

Ferdinand de Lesseps, the constructor of the Suez Canal, happened to be related to Eugénie – his mother was Spanish, an aunt of Eugénie's mother. He started his career as a diplomat, and was French Consul in Cairo and Alexandria, where he became very friendly with Said Pacha, the son of the Viceroy of Egypt. When Said Pacha became Viceroy in 1854, de Lesseps approached his old friend with a scheme for a canal linking the Mediterranean with the Red Sea.

Thanks to the enthusiastic support of Napoleon III and Eugénie, the French public soon raised more than half the necessary capital. In 1859, de Lesseps himself dug the first spadeful of sand. The canal was opened on 18 November 1869 before a glittering array of European royalty, headed by the Empress Eugénie *right*

Roger-Viollet

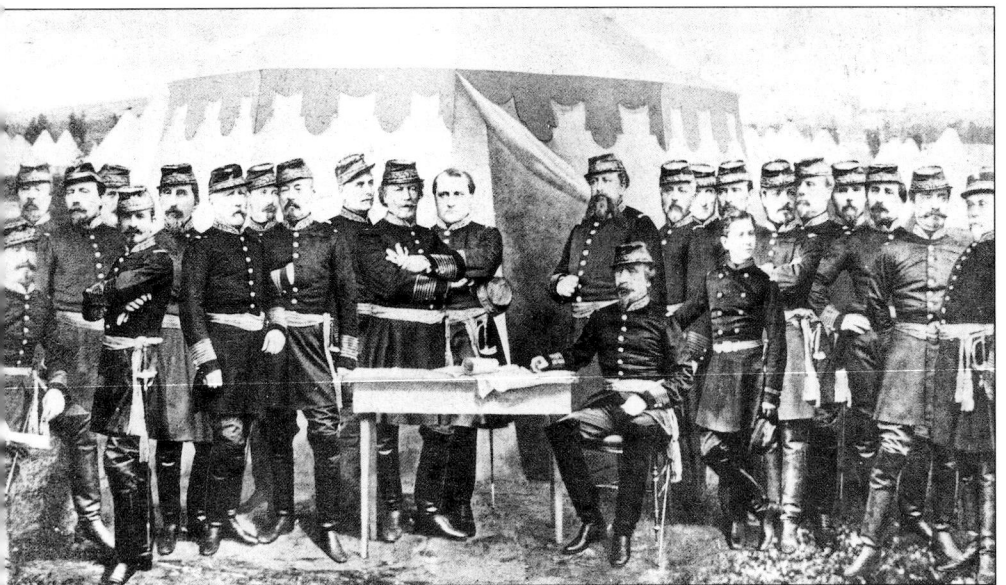

♔ *France declared war on Prussia in 1870 to try to curb the growth of German influence in Europe. When the Emperor and his son joined his chiefs-of-staff* above, *hopes were high, but soon after he was obliged to welcome King William of Prussia on to French soil* below, inset. *Napoleon was taken to Wilhelmshöhe in Prussia; the telegram* below *records his arrival at the castle*

Background picture: Popperfoto/Inset: Jean-Loup Charmet

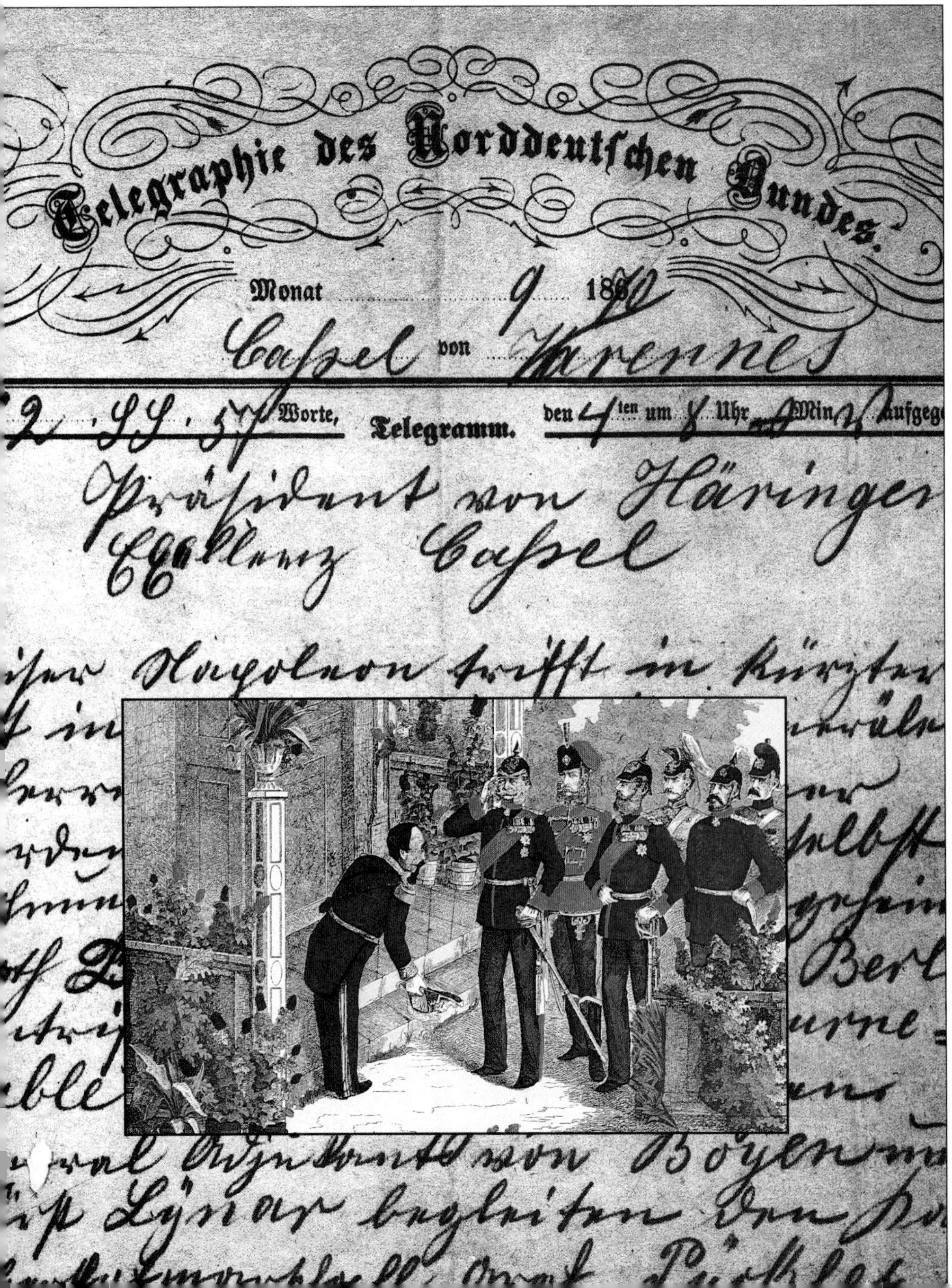

front, there were only 220,000. The first major defeat came on 4 August. Others soon followed. The various armies in eastern France did not know whether to retreat or stay where they were. The presence of the Emperor only made things worse.

Eugénie in charge

In Paris, Eugénie, whom Napoleon had appointed Regent, dismissed Ollivier and appointed the veteran General Palikao in his place. But it was really the Empress herself who now governed France, staying up half the night with the aid of black coffee, poring over the despatches received at the Palace and sending new and confusing ones to her husband and the generals in the field.

Preparations were made for the defence of Paris. Napoleon suggested that General Bazaine's army around Metz should fall back to the French military camp at Châlons, but Eugénie telegraphed that public opinion would not accept a retreat on top of the recent defeats.

Louis left Bazaine, now appointed commander-in-chief at Metz, and returned to Châlons with his son. There, urged by his cousin, Prince Napoleon, to take some decisive action, he said that he would have to consult Eugénie first. This prompted the question: who was ruling France? To which the weary Emperor replied pathetically, 'I seem to have abdicated.'

> ***'I never dreamt of a catastrophe so appalling'***
>
> LOUIS AT SEDAN

Death before dishonour

A liberal ally of Prince Napoleon, General Trochu, was sent back to Paris to act as Military Governor. This infuriated Eugénie, who could not countermand the Emperor's order. Her communications to her husband grew increasingly hysterical: he must not dishonour the family name by abandoning his armies. Even 30 years later, the Empress was still convinced that this had been the correct advice: 'Leave his troops on the eve of battle! He, a Napoleon! He would have covered himself with shame before history for ever more! I would rather he had killed himself!'

Napoleon decided that the Prince Imperial should be sent to safety. He was entrusted to three aides, who managed, by a dangerous and roundabout route, to bring him to England.

The Emperor himself joined the army of General MacMahon at Sedan. His own descrip-

Lauros-Giraudon

tion of the position was: 'I never dreamt of a catastrophe so appalling. Just imagine an army surrounding a fortified city and itself surrounded on every side by forces far superior.'

Capitulation

The Germans attacked on 1 September. Louis had no command, but he remained in the saddle for five hours, riding round encouraging the troops. A surgeon, familiar with his bladder trouble, later supposed that 'The agony must have been constant.' There was no hope for the outnumbered French; Louis ordered the white flag to be raised and wrote to the King of Prussia: 'Having been unable to die in the midst of my troops, it only remains for me to place my sword in Your Majesty's hands. I am Your Majesty's good brother, Napoleon.'

Louis Napoleon was taken prisoner. He spoke with Bismarck and with King William, then was conveyed to Germany, to the castle of Wilhelmshöhe, near Kassel. The Second Empire had met its Waterloo. In Paris, when a telegram arrived with news of the surrender, Eugénie refused to believe it: 'A Napoleon never surrenders! He is dead! I tell you he is dead!'

Eugénie flees

Eugénie had worked gallantly in the interest of her country, organizing the defences of Paris and converting part of the Tuileries into a military hospital. Now all her work counted for nothing. The fickle Paris mob was once again a re-

publican mob. On 4 September, her ministers told her she would have to leave Paris.

Richard Metternich and the Italian ambassador helped Eugénie escape from the Palace, but then she and her companion, Mme Lebreton, her reader, became separated from their rescuers. The man they were relying on to help them was not at home and they had spent their last money on a cab-ride. When Mme Lebreton suggested they seek safety in the American Embassy, Eugénie realized there was one last hope. The Empress of the French rang the doorbell of Dr Evans, an American dentist.

👑 *Prussia's swift and comprehensive defeat of France sent shock waves around Europe. The Second Empire was in ruins, and the once-powerful French army was destroyed, desolate and demoralized* above

👑 *Nothing was left for Napoleon and his family but exile in England, at Chislehurst* below. *The ordeal did not last long for Louis, who had less than two years to live*

Roger-Viollet

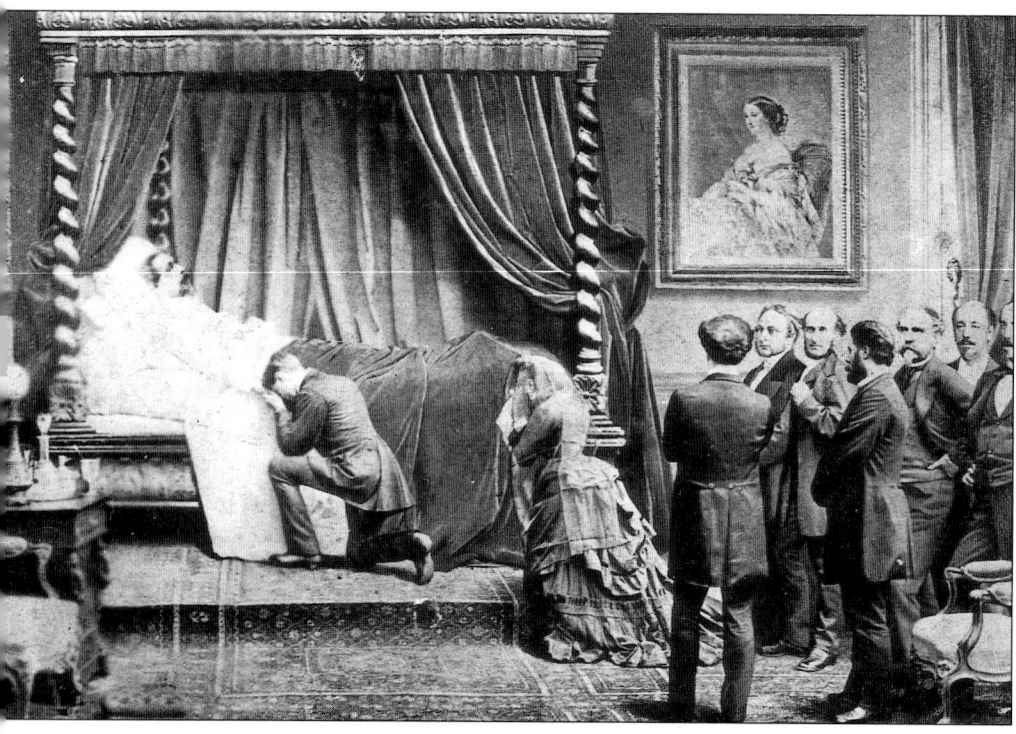

Popperfoto

👑 *The end came for Louis on 9 January 1873 when, despite the attendance of several fine physicians, he succumbed to peritonitis caused by the bladder stone that had afflicted him, undiagnosed, for years. He died at Camden Place, beneath one of Winterhalter's pictures of the young Empress, with his wife and son at his side* above

'I should like to go to England and live with you and Louis in a little cottage'

NAPOLEON III

ESCAPE FROM FRANCE

Dr Evans proved quite equal to the task of smuggling the two ladies to safety in England. Using a succession of highly unsuitable horse-drawn vehicles and at one point taking a train, he and a friend, Dr Crane, conducted their heavily-veiled 'nervous patient' to Deauville on the Normandy coast. In the neighbouring harbour of Trouville, Evans found a yacht belonging to Sir John Burgoyne, who rather reluctantly agreed to ferry them across the Channel to safety in England.

Eugénie's fantastic journey ended happily. At the Imperial Hotel, Hastings, she was reunited with her son. When she saw her husband again it was also a joyful reunion. Despite the violent differences of opinion over the last few years, their suffering had brought them together. Louis' letters from Wilhelmshöhe were full of affection. 'When I am free,' he wrote, 'I should like to go to England, and live with you and Louis in a little cottage with bow-windows and a creeper.' Eugénie was able to pay him a surprise visit at the end of October. All was forgiven.

Court in exile

In England, Eugénie had rented a house, Camden Place in Chislehurst. Queen Victoria, who visited her old friend there, referred to its 'humble little rooms', but there were at least 20 of them. It was a sizeable house. Hostilities between the French and the Germans ended on 29 January 1871. The siege of Paris was lifted and King William of Prussia became Emperor of Germany. The Emperor of the French was allowed to leave Wilhelmshöhe on 19 March.

Louis was astonished at the friendly reception he received in England. Despite their close ties with the Prussian Royal Family, Queen Victoria and the Prince of Wales made him and Eugénie very welcome.

One of the deposed couple's first problems was money – Louis prided himself on being one of the few deposed rulers not to have deposited government funds in a foreign bank. Fortunately, Pauline Metternich had been entrusted with some of Eugénie's fabulous collection of jewellery, which she had duly delivered to Camden Place. The sale of the jewels brought them £60,000, plenty to be getting on with.

Life at Camden Place was quiet, but politics were not forgotten. Bonapartists still gathered round their Emperor, taking tea under the cedar tree on the lawn. Events in France – the founding of the Paris Commune and the establishment of the Third Republic – were discussed endlessly and vague plans made for the future. But Louis and Eugénie knew in their hearts that there was no future. Louis accepted his fate with stoic resignation.

The Emperor dies

Eugénie would say afterwards, 'You should have seen him in his last years at Chislehurst: never a word of complaint, of blame or recrimination.' But the pain in Louis' bladder got worse and the seemingly incessant English rain brought on attacks of rheumatism. The end came, after two unsuccessful operations, on 9 January 1873.

Roger-Viollet

👑 *Eugénie and her son lived on at Chislehurst after Louis' death. Young Napoleon became an army cadet left and it was rumoured that he would marry Queen Victoria's youngest daughter, Beatrice*

Reunion Musees Nationaux

Roger-Viollet

👑 *Young Louis above, styled Napoleon IV after his father's death, was not content to wait his country's call in exile. Craving excitement, he went with the British army to Africa, where his patrol was surprised by Zulus. His gun arm was injured when a strap broke as he attempted to vault into the saddle. He fought on but was overwhelmed and pierced by 18 assegais*

Eugénie's grief at the death of her husband was restrained compared to what she had felt at the death of her father or her sister. Far greater grief was to still to come. The Prince Imperial, who had become a cadet at the Military Academy at Woolwich, might yet live to be Napoleon IV. The Empress kept him on a tight rein, fearing he might have inherited some of his father's less admirable characteristics. Young Louis naturally got bored.

👑 *Eugénie lived on alone, becoming the doyenne of the Royal Families of Europe. She divided her time between her homes in Britain and France and her yacht Thistle where, as an old lady in her eighties, she was visited by Kaiser Wilhelm II of Germany, the grandson of the man whose armies had broken her husband right*

Jean-Loup Charmet

'I cannot even die'

EUGÉNIE

👑 *In the year of her death, aged 94, Eugénie visited the Queen of Spain and her birthplace above*

For a time he enjoyed the delights of London with the Prince of Wales, and there was even a rumour of his getting engaged to Queen Victoria's youngest daughter, Beatrice, but this was not what he really wanted. He had trained as a soldier and he wanted to see action.

Death and vindication

In 1879 Louis begged to be allowed to join an expedition to fight the Zulus. His mother relented and arranged, with the help of Queen Victoria, for the War Office to let him serve in the British Army. He sailed for Cape Town on 27 February. On 1 June, on a reconnaissance mission into Zulu territory, he was killed.

Eugénie was completely devastated: 'I cannot even die; and God, in his infinite mercy, will give me a hundred years of life.' She very nearly did live a hundred years. People thought her sons's death would send her into a decline, but the following year she set out on a pilgrimage to the spot where he had been killed, calling in on the way at another Napoleonic shrine – the island of St. Helena.

From Chislehurst she moved to Farnborough, where she could build a memorial to her husband and son. She later bought some land on the French Riviera at Cap Martin, where she built the Villa Cyrnos. Much of the time, however, she spent not at either of her two homes, but on board her yacht, *The Thistle*, which she had bought in 1889. She lived long enough to see her husband's defeat at Sedan revenged by the victory of France and England in the First World War. She died, aged 94, on 21 July 1920.

FARNBOROUGH HILL

For almost 40 years, the Hampshire town of Farnborough was the home of the former Empress of the French. After the deaths of her husband and son, Eugénie decided to move from Kent. She found Farnborough Hill, a 23-roomed Victorian gothic mansion set in a magnificent park, and bought it in 1881. The house was not large enough for Eugénie's purpose – her collection of Napoleonic memorabilia had grown to enormous size – so a new wing of 18 rooms was added.

She renamed the park 'Compiègne' and in it she had built an abbey and a mausoleum to house the remains of her husband and her son. Her wandering life often took her away from Farnborough, but with the outbreak of the Great War, she was forced to live in England. Happy to play her part in avenging the defeat at Sedan, she agreed that part of the house *right* could be used as a hospital for officers wounded in action in France